IN THE EVER AFTER

IN THE EVER AFTER

Fairy Tales and the Second Half of Life

Allan B. Chinen

Chiron Publications • Wilmette, Illinois

Third printing, 1992

Library of Congress catalog Card Number: 88 – 28826.

Printed in the United States of America.
Edited by Michael McNett
Book design by April Lemke.

Library of Congress Cataloging-in-Publication Data:
Chinen, Allan B., 1952-
     In the ever after : fairy tales and the second half of life / Allan B. Chinen.
        p. cm.
     Bibliography: p.
     Includes index.
     1. Old age—Folklore. 2. Fairy tales. 3. Psychoanalysis and folklore. I. Title.
GR 488.C48 1989
398'.354—dc19   88 – 28826
                                                                                    CIP

ISBN 0-933029-41-1 (paper)

Dedicated to my mother and father, in their elder years.

Contents

Acknowledgments

The many friends and colleagues who have encouraged me with this book are too numerous to thank individually. But I particularly want to express my appreciation to those people who lent their aid and counsel at crucial moments in this long project—the fairy godmothers and godfathers of this book: Bruce Baker for his sage advice; John Boe, for his insightful and stimulating comments; James and Rosalie Heacock, for believing when few did; Gisela Labouvie-Vief, for her knowledge and vision of the second half of life; and Miles Vich, for the first break. I also want to thank the Robert Wood Johnson Clinical Scholars Program and the Ella Lyman Cabot Trust for their generous financial support which made the research possible. And finally, I am deeply grateful to all the forgotten storytellers who first told elder tales, long ago, bequeathing us their rich legacy of wisdom.

1
Introduction

Handed down over the centuries, fairy tales are rich treasures of human wisdom, distilling the observations and reflections of many generations. As Bruno Bettelheim points out in his popular book, *The Uses of Enchantment*, apparently simple stories like "Snow White" and "Little Red Riding Hood" contain important insights about human psychology.[1] Indeed, fairy tales are parables of the human journey through life, as Marie-Louise von Franz discusses in her delightful series of books.[2]

In most familiar stories the protagonists are children, like Little Red Riding Hood or at most an adolescent, like Cinderella. Not surprisingly, interpretations of these fairy tales have emphasized the psychology of youth, and focused on the tasks of growing up. In the typical drama, a child or youth sometimes voluntarily leaves home, seeking better fortune in the world, as in "Thom Thumb," or is involuntarily thrown out of the house, as in "Hansel and Gretel." The departure represents a major task of adolescence, when each individual must separate from his or her parents to begin an independent life. The process is rarely easy in the real world, and so fairy tales depict their protagonists struggling through many ordeals—fighting witches or outwitting giants. Eventually, the young hero or heroine wins a kingdom and finds true love, symbolizing what most individuals achieve in real life—they "find themselves," take a place in society, and make commitments to spouse and career. Most fairy tales end at this point with the youthful dream of happiness so charmingly summed up by the phrase, "and they lived happily ever after."

Real life, of course, does not end with youth or eternal happiness. So a question naturally arises: What happens in the "ever after," when the hero and heroine have children of their own, and white hair crowns the Prince and Princess?

The question is not merely whimsical. Fairy tales portray timeless paradigms of human life, and often mirror the scripts which individuals play out in their lives—as psychoanalysts and mythologists have observed.[3] One youth may flirt with danger and climb mountains, seeking to live out the hero's adventure. Another may move restlessly from relationship to relationship, yearning for the perfect lover—the fairy tale Prince or Princess. And the dream of living happily ever after is a singularly powerful motivation in youth. Its spell is so entrancing that it is usually never questioned—until the individual finally arrives at the "ever after" sometime in mid-life and is rudely awakened.

What happens next? A distinctive group of fairy stories provides some of the answers. These tales feature protagonists who are explicitly called "old," so these stories may be called "elder tales." They contrast with more familiar stories like "Cinderella" or "Snow White" which focus on young characters and which can be called "youth tales." But the definition of "old" and "young" requires some caution.

From scattered hints, it seems that fairy tales call people "young" if they are teenagers or children, while anyone over forty or fifty is "old." This will no doubt horrify most readers, because fifty is no longer considered "old." But fairy tales originated long ago, when life was harsh—and short. The average life expectancy in medieval Europe was less than 25. So someone of 40 years was counted long-lived, and a person of 60, miraculously old.[4] In fairy tales, then, the word "old" really means "middle-aged and beyond."

The thesis of this book is that fairy tales about "old" protagonists reveal the psychology of maturity. Elder tales symbolize the developmental tasks individuals must master in the second half of life, just as youth tales symbolize the tasks of the first. Elder tales do not speak of growing *up*, they deal instead with growing

2

old, and most importantly, with *growing*—psychologically and spiritually.

Of course, older men and women appear in virtually all fairy tales, but in most familiar stories, older individuals usually play secondary roles. They are cast as the wicked old woman, like the evil stepmother in "Snow White," or appear as the unbelievably good person, like the fairy godmother in "Cinderella." Tales in which the older person is a realistic *protagonist* are distinctly less common. Indeed from over 4,000 fairy tales reviewed for this book, only about 2 percent are "elder tales."[5]

By "fairy tale," I should explain, I mean a specific kind of story—a folk tale with a happy ending, featuring ordinary people in fantastic situations, struggling with basic human dilemmas. Each of these features is worth elaborating upon because together they explain why fairy tales are both appealing and insightful. First of all, as scholars from different disciplines emphasize,[6] fairy tales are traditional stories handed down through the ages. Through being told and retold so many times by so many people, purely personal elements and cultural idiosyncracies tend to be washed away, leaving dramas and insights of universal interest. Indeed, this is probably one reason that fairy tales from around the world are surprisingly similar—the Cinderella story, for instance, can be found in Europe, Asia, and Africa. And the same holds true of elder tales. As we shall see, similar stories come from diverse cultures.

Authentic fairy tales thus contrast with "literary" stories written by individual authors—stories like *The Wind in the Willows, Winnie the Pooh,* or the tales of Hans Christian Andersen. Fairy tales by individual authors usually reflect the psychology of that person, while folk stories reflect that of mankind in general.

Fairy tales also do not claim to be true and quickly tell us that,[7] typically starting off with comments like, "When wishing still worked," or "When clothes still grew on the clothes tree."[8] They differ therefore from myths and legends which demand belief. Indeed, what we call "myths" today were the religious revelations of yesterday, and "legends" the historical truths. The Greeks prayed to Zeus and Apollo and did not merely study them in mythology class. By contrast, fairy tales take us away from belief and explicitly draw us into a realm of fantasy. This, paradoxically, is the strength of the genre. Through imagination, fairy tales portray what *can* be, and not what simply *is*. They break the bonds of practical reality and social convention, and offer a vision of human ideals and ideal human development— hence the happy endings characteristic of fairy tales, which distinguish them from horror stories or tragedies.[9] The optimism of fairy tales is not mere sentimentality, but an expression of humanity's deepest and highest hopes.

Yet fairy tales focus on *ordinary people,*[10] characters who are intensely human and filled with the same fears and foolishness as any modern man or woman. So fairy tale protagonists are easy to identify with, in contrast to the gods and heros of myths. This makes the insights of fairy tales psychologically accessible because the ideals the stories portray are the ones to which most people aspire. For elder tales, those ideals involve the second half of life. So the stories essentially offer a vision of what life *can* be in the middle and later years.

Today more than ever, we need such ideals. With advances in public health, the economic standard of living, and medical practice, individuals can expect to live to a ripe old age. This is the celebrated "greying" of America, and most adults undoubtedly plan for it, investing money, exercising regularly, and eating right. But a basic question still remains, captured in the title of the award-winning book by Robert Butler, former president of the Gerontological Society of America—*Why Survive?*[11] What is the meaning and purpose of living so long?

In today's society, most ideals of human life revolve around images of youth—strength and beauty, for instance. These are the virtues of the hero and heroine, so closely associated with youth. Without any vision of what succeeds youth and its heroic paradigm, the second half of life often seems frightful, a time only of deterioration. No one has captured this horrifying view better than Simone de Beauvoir in her devastating critique of ageism, *The Coming of Age.*[12] In a society centered around youth, the older individual is caught between the specter of decline and the dream of eternal youth. Despair is usually the victor. As Mimnermus, a 7th century B.C. Greek wrote, capturing an almost universal fear of old age, "The fruit of youth rots early; it barely lasts as long as the light of day. And once it is over, life is worse than death."[13]

Elder tales offer a dramatic alternative to this grim view—a new image of maturity, centered around wisdom, self-knowledge, and transcendence. These are the virtues, as we shall see, of an archetypal figure long overlooked in modern society, but equal in importance to that of the Hero—the Elder.

The rarity of elder tales raises a question: If the stories contain vital insights, why have they been so neglected? Here lies a tale in its own right—a tale of elder tales.

Elder tales are more common in Eastern cultures, like those of Japan, Arabia, India, and China. One reason is that these cultures accord older adults more respect than modern Western society and so naturally put a larger number of older people in their folktales. But we cannot settle for this simple explanation. In the past, Western culture also respected older adults. In the Bible, for instance, longevity was taken to be a sign of God's grace, and biblical kings lived to fabulous ages. So other factors must work to make elder tales obscure.

In the "olden days," when society was based on agriculture, age and experience were invaluable assets. The old farmer knew when to hasten harvesting, noting the clues that winter would come early—the squirrels had thicker fur, perhaps, or the birds began migrating sooner than expected. The young farmer would not know such subtle warnings. In agricultural societies, too, old people were the ones who usually owned land and so wielded great economic power. They accordingly appeared in folklore more frequently, and with greater reverence.[14] With the emergence of modern industry, and its rapidly evolving technology, the knowledge of older adults quickly became obsolete. And with industrialization, ownership of land became less important than the ability to learn new skills quickly. Eventually the older person became obsolete in society and was portrayed that way in fairy tales.[15]

If older persons began to seem unimportant, fairy tales soon did too. The connection between the two should not be surprising because older adults are traditionally the ones who tell stories. (Even today, stories are remembered better if the tale is told by an old person rather than a middle-aged or younger one.)[16] And long ago, folktales played the roles of newspaper, television, and library, providing news, entertainment, and education. They were invaluable resources—until the advent of books. Since written information is more accurate than personal memory, folktales began to seem "backward" and "old-fashioned," like witchcraft and other superstitions. But fairy tales could not be ignored completely; they address issues that are too important to overlook, problems with which each generation must deal, in every culture. So fairy tales were exiled to the nursery rather than eliminated completely, and folk wisdom degenerated into children's entertainment.[17] Many elder tales were lost in the process, and those that remain to this day are survivors, a point I shall discuss later.

To reclaim these forgotten tales for modern readers, I have chosen stories which are typical of elder tales, and retold them, trying to remain true to their original intuitions. Some people may object to this retelling, preferring the original versions, but there were several reasons for the adaptations. In some cases, the original versions used languages such as Old English which are no longer relevant. Other stories were so condensed that they were difficult to enjoy; they were more like synopses than real fairy tales. Still more tales were written at length in simple language aimed at children rather than adults. Most important of all, as oral folklore, fairy tales are supposed to be told from one person to another, and adapted to different circumstances. There is no single "right" version.[18] So instead of apologizing for retelling the stories, I encourage readers to tell them in their turn, in their way, the better to experience and understand the stories. I indicate the sources of the original versions for those interested. Most stories come from several independent references, handed down over the centuries, and known by many different people, underscoring their authentic folk origins.

In interpreting the elder tales in this volume, I rely upon psychodynamic theories of human development—particularly those of Carl Jung and Erik Erikson, updated by recent research in aging. More than other psychoanalysts, Jung and Erikson initiated the psychological study of adult development, and while most of their work was intuitive and based on personal experiences with individuals in psychotherapy, subsequent research with large numbers of people has proven many of their observations to be correct—as we shall discuss.

Psychoanalysts have pointed out that fairy tales are very much like dreams, and can be interpreted in a similar manner. The analogy is a happy one. Both dreams and tales use symbols—the language of unconscious imagination, rather than of conscious reason—and they address matters of the soul and not merely the mind. Moreover, when taken alone, a single dream may not make much sense. But in a series, recurrent themes quickly emerge and serve as keys to the dream symbolism. Elder tales are no different. Any single story may simply be a charming tale, with little deeper meaning. Indeed, interpretations are precarious if they are based on only one tale. As scholars of folklore have pointed out, many psychoanalytic commentaries have been based on a detail present in one version of a tale, and absent in all others.[19] When elder tales are assembled together, however, as they are here for the first time, similar themes stand out. By comparing elder tales with each other, and with fairy stories about youth, more secure interpretations are possible.

The analogy with dreams emphasizes another point about interpreting fairy tales: their historical and cultural milieu cannot be ignored. Just as dreams reflect the personality and life events of the dreamer, so are fairy tales influenced by their social contexts. Comparing elder tales from different cultures is thus essential if we are to extract universal insights from them.

Unless the wisdom of dreams can be applied to waking life, however, dreaming is fruitless. And the same holds true for elder tales. But real people struggle with the same problems as the characters in elder tales—and come to similar solutions. Whether they are older men and women in psychotherapy, or historical figures from different cultures, individuals in real life confirm the wisdom of elder tales. Reality mirrors fantasy. And systematic research on aging corroborates many of the insights of elder tales, as I shall discuss. Indeed, in some cases, modern research is only now catching up with the wisdom in fairy tales.

Ultimately, the validity of any interpretation depends on its authenticity. Does the interpretation of a story ring true? Does it awaken forgotten wisdom and inspire new hope? Questions like these can only be answered by each individual, reflecting pri-

7

vately on the stories, and then on their own lives. In the succeeding pages, I append a few interpretive comments after each tale to provide a springboard for reflection, and at the conclusion of the book, I summarize and integrate the many different themes. Taken together, I argue, elder tales present a coherent psychological map of the tasks individuals must negotiate in the second half of life—warning of the difficulties and dangers, and previewing the promise and potential.

Elder tales are paradoxical. Like any other fairy tale, they entertain children with magic, suspense, drama, and inspiration. Yet elder tales also address the concerns of mature adults, struggling with the psychological tasks of later life. So elder tales are tailored to the modern fairy tale situation—the parent or grandparent telling stories to children. Elder tales entertain one and advise the other, combining childlike innocence with deep psychological insight. That astonishing union, as we shall see, is the central promise of elder tales. Magic and innocence return in the second half of life, uniting the beginning with the end, transfiguring "the ever after."

2

Fortune and the Woodcutter

(a tale from Asia Minor)

nce upon a time, there lived an old wood-
cutter with his wife. He labored each day
in the forest, from dawn to dusk, cutting wood to sell in the
village. But no matter how hard he struggled, he could not
succeed in life, and what he earned in the day, he and his
family ate up at night. Two sons soon brightened his hearth,
and they worked by his side. Father and sons cut three times
the wood, and earned three times the money, but they ate
three times the food, too, and so the woodcutter was no better off than before. Then the young men left home to seek
their own fortunes.

After twenty years, the old man finally had enough.
"I've worked for Fortune all my life," he exclaimed to his
wife, "and she has given us little enough for it. From now
on," the old man swore, "if Fortune wants to give us anything, she will have to come looking for me." And the woodcutter vowed to work no more.

"Good heavens," his wife cried out, "if you don't work,
we won't eat! And what are you saying? Fortune visits great
sultans, not poor folk like us!" But no matter how much she
tried to persuade him—and she reasoned, cried, and yelled—
the old woodcutter refused to work. In fact, he decided to
stay in bed.

Later that day, a stranger came knocking at the door, and asked if he could borrow the old man's mules for a few hours. The stranger explained that he had some work to do in the forest, and that he noticed the woodcutter was not using his mules. The old man agreed, still lounging in bed. He simply asked the stranger to feed and water the two animals.

The stranger then took the mules deep into the forest. He was no ordinary man, but a magician, and through his arts, he had learned where a great treasure lay. So he went to the spot and dug up heaps of gold and jewels, loading the booty on the two mules. But just as he prepared to leave, gloating over his new wealth, soldiers came marching down the road. The stranger became frightened. He knew that if the soldiers found him with the treasure, they would ask questions. His sorcery would be discovered and he would be condemned to death. So the stranger fled into the forest and was never seen or heard from again.

The soldiers went along their way, noticing nothing unusual, and so the two mules waited undisturbed in the forest. After many hours, they started for home on their own, following the trails they had used with the woodcutter for many years.

When they arrived at the woodcutter's home, his wife saw the poor animals. She ran upstairs. "Dear husband," she cried out, "come quickly. You must unload the mules before they collapse!"

The husband yawned and turned over in bed. "If I've told you once, I've told you a thousand times. I'm not working anymore."

The poor woman hurried downstairs, thought for a second, and then fetched a kitchen knife. She ran to the mules and slashed the bags on their backs to lighten the load. Gold and jewels poured out, flashing in the sun.

"Gold! Jewels!" she exclaimed. In a flash, her husband was downstairs, and he stared in astonishment at the trea-

10

sure spilling into their yard. Then he grabbed his wife and they danced deliriously. "Fortune did come to us after all!" he exulted.

And when the old man and his wife gave half their treasure to their sons, and half the remainder to the poor, they were still as rich as rich could be!

Summarized from "Fortune and the Woodcutter," in A. Lang, The Brown Fairy Book *(London: Longmans, Green, 1914); a similar story, "Allah Will Provide," can be found in R. Gilstrap and I. Estabrook,* The Sultan's Fool and Other North African Tales *(New York: Holt, Rinehart and Winston, 1958).*

Reflections: Loss and the Return of Magic

This story is enchanting, and on the surface, it might seem like any other fairy tale, with magical events and a happy ending. But if we look closely, there are several unusual details which reappear in other elder tales, and which symbolize important insights about psychological development in the second half of life.

The story introduces us to a man who has married, raised his children, seen them leave, and worked at a trade for "twenty years." In the days when the average life expectancy was often less than thirty, as mentioned before, twenty years of work would put the woodcutter well into the second half of life. So his story begins where tales of youth end—in the ever after. Instead of living happily though, the woodcutter and his wife live alone in dreadful poverty. Elder tales typically begin with this dismal situation, suggesting that the theme is significant.

One possibility is that the poverty simply depicts historical reality: work, we might think, was physically demanding back then, and old individuals unable to keep up were quickly impoverished. Surprisingly, this was not generally true. For one thing, adults who survived to old age in those days were often quite robust.[1] And in traditional cultures older persons had important skills, knowledge, and social authority which would ease their burden. However, historical truth is not the issue here. Fairy tales,

11

like dreams, are figurative rather than literal, and dreams usually start with events from real life, only to add on important symbolic meanings. In a similar way, fairy tales use historical realities, but then work in deeper insights.

Poverty is deprivation, and so connotes *loss*. Poverty thus makes a good symbol in elder tales for the losses of aging: the loss of health, of loved ones, or of financial security. In today's society, pensions may protect older adults from outright poverty, and modern medicine offers some buffer against premature death, but other losses remain—beauty, strength, intellectual agility, and often friends, who die before their time. Indeed, even in cultures which venerate elders, and where adults exaggerate their age for purposes of prestige, the infirmities of old age are greatly feared.

Elder tales start out by recognizing these fears in symbolic form. This presents a challenge to us, because most adults dismiss fairy tales for their unrealistic, upbeat views of life. By beginning with a sobering picture of loss, elder tales force us to think twice about their message.

This second look is important. All too often, adults dismiss the possibility of "happy endings" in later life, and resign themselves to a slow decline. But this is simply a symptom of depression, which afflicts many individuals in the second half of life, up to 30 percent in some surveys.[2] Depression often goes unrecognized, though, because its symptoms take on new forms in later life. In youth, depression typically involves feelings of sadness or guilt, while in maturity, the symptoms frequently take the form of forgetfulness, lack of energy, apathy, and psychosomatic ailments, which are easily dismissed as the inevitable price of aging. Indeed, many depressed older individuals are mistakenly thought to be senile, although their memory problems improve when the depression is adequately treated.[3]

On a deeper level, then, the poverty in "Fortune and the Woodcutter" symbolizes depression. The problem obviously occurs in youth, too, but young men and women at least have the consolation of the future and the hope that coming years can make up for their misfortunes. Not so in the second half of life, when time runs out. So if the psychological wisdom of the elder tale applies to all ages, later life is still the setting of greatest need.

One detail deserves further notice. The old woodcutter is a

healthy man, and in general, the protagonists of elder tales are quite vigorous. Are elder tales therefore unrealistic, given the many ailments of later life? Here we can follow a general principle in interpreting dreams and fairy tales: physical conditions often symbolize psychological states. We can therefore construe the physical health portrayed in elder tales to be symbols of *psychological* health, and particularly, of emotional maturity. These stories, after all, take up where youth tales leave off—after the individual has developed a sense of self, and learned to cope with the world, and both those achievements require a sturdy, adaptable ego.

If most adults anticipate old age as a dismal time, asking, "What else can I expect?" the story of "Fortune and the Woodcutter" provides a refreshing answer: a lot. Indeed the tale suggests, with the poet Robert Browning, that "the best is yet to be."

In the story, the old woodcutter resolves not to work anymore, and his decision is astonishing, especially if we compare it to tales of youth. In the latter, the young hero or heroine must leave home to find better fortune, and initiative is required of them. By contrast, the old woodcutter ventures nowhere, and instead settles down comfortably in bed, of all places. He becomes extraordinarily passive. What might this event symbolize?

An easy interpretation is that the woodcutter has a tantrum; his hope that Fortune will come to him is simply wishful thinking, no different from daydreaming. As with most fairy tales, wishful thinking is certainly one level of significance, but there are deeper meanings. Fairy tales appeal to us precisely because they tantalize our childish desires, while hinting at more profound truths.

The old man's idleness is unique in several ways. First he *chooses* not to work. In youth tales, by contrast, if the hero does not work it is simply because he knows no trade. He is idle from ignorance, not choice. Second, the old woodcutter must resist his wife's pleas to work. And since working was the woodcutter's life for so many years, sudden leisure would no doubt be psychologically difficult (as is the case with many individuals today who retire without any preparation for the change). So the woodcutter's inaction is paradoxically quite active—he must work to preserve his leisure. In effect, he clears the way for something new to emerge in his life. If he followed his usual routine, his mules would not have been available for the stranger to use, and nothing further would have evolved.

The story quickly takes us to its surprising events. The stranger finds a treasure and loads it on the old man's mules. But then the stranger flees and the mules return home by themselves, bringing Fortune to the old man. Here lies the major theme of this story and elder tales in general: magic returns in the second half of life, and it occurs when least expected, in the midst of poverty. What are we to make of such magic?

Possibly, we are dealing again with wishful thinking and daydreaming. However, consider the importance of one detail: the mules. For all his powers, the stranger apparently cannot obtain the treasure without the beasts. They have been trained by the woodcutter and used by him through many years of labor. So they represent his hard work and skill. And the mules return home by themselves only because they have followed the same trail many times before. Fortune comes to the old man *because he worked with his mules for many years.* So his Fortune is more like the return on an investment than a magic gift. (Indeed, this tale can be construed as a story of successful retirement.) Notice, too, how the magic in this elder tale differs from that in tales of youth. There magic simply happens, effortlessly and with no preconditions. The young man or woman is freely given help by a fairy godmother, or some magical creature, and such generosity reflects the naive optimism and wishful hopes of youth.

The return of magic in later life is not merely the stuff of older tales. It happens frequently in real life. One businessman of my acquaintance, for instance, suffered a major heart attack in his early 60's which forced him to retire from work. In his unexpected—and enforced—leisure time, he took up painting, an activity he had enjoyed as an adolescent, but forgotten. To his own surprise, and that of his family and colleagues, this hard-driving businessman thoroughly enjoyed painting. He quickly became highly skilled at it, partly because he applied years of self-discipline to his new vocation. Magic returned unexpectedly to his life in the form of creativity and beauty. And John McLeish, in his book *The Ulyssean Adult,*[4] presents even more dramatic examples—from Cervantes, the creator of Don Quixote, who turned from soldiering to writing in his 60's, to Wilder Penfield, who became a successful novelist after a distinguished career as a neurosurgeon.

The exact nature of the magic in the second half of life remains unclear in the present elder tale. To understand the symbolism more fully, we must look to other stories for explanation and corroboration. And this will be a general strategy I will follow throughout the book: the questions one elder tale raises, others will answer. By themselves, individual tales are incomplete. They must be assembled together, like the pieces of a puzzle. Only then does the overall pattern emerge.

3

The Sparrow's Gift

(from Japan)

ong ago and far away, an old woman lived with her husband at the edge of a forest. The old man was kind-hearted and kept a sparrow as a pet, playing with the little bird each morning and evening. He fed the sparrow tidbits from his own plate and sang songs to it. His wife, for her part, complained constantly about the creature. "It is noisy! It eats too much! It dirties the house!" she grumbled. None of this was true, but the old woman complained about everything under the sun.

One day, the old man went to work in his fields. His wife made some starch for her laundry and went to fetch her clothes. But when she returned, the starch was gone. She cursed and complained and the little sparrow came flying down. It spread its wings, bowed to the old woman, and then said, "I am sorry, I ate the starch. But I thought it was for me!"

The old woman was enraged to hear this. "You eat everything in the house!" she swore at the bird, and said many worse things. Then in a fit of anger, she grabbed the poor creature with one hand, and a pair of scissors with the other, and she cut the bird's tongue off. "Let's see you eat without a tongue!" the old woman cried out, "and chirp so cheerfully!" The poor bird flew away, moaning in pain.

That evening, the old man returned home. When the sparrow did not greet him, he became concerned, and when the bird did not answer his calls, he became alarmed. "It must have flown away," his wife said, "such an ungrateful thing! After all the kindness we showed it." The old man did not believe his wife and he pestered her with questions. Finally she told him what happened.

"Oh no!" the old man exclaimed in horror, "you cut off her tongue!" He wanted to run outside to search for the poor bird, but it was night by then and he knew it would be useless to look in the dark. So he waited till morning, and as soon as dawn came, he hurried to the woods, whistling and calling for the sparrow. A few minutes later, the bird fluttered down from a bamboo grove. The old man apologized profusely for what his wife had done, and asked if the bird needed any help.

"Please don't worry," the sparrow said and smiled. The old man saw the little bird had grown a new tongue. "Let me take you to my home in the woods," the sparrow invited the old man. And so he followed her deep into the forest. There he came upon the most beautiful house he had ever seen and he knew immediately that his pet was no ordinary sparrow, but a fairy.

The sparrow introduced the old man to all her family, and they brought out a wonderful meal for him to eat. The sparrow's daughters danced and played music and the old man enjoyed himself so much, he did not notice the time passing. Then he saw the sun low on the horizon. "Oh dear," he exclaimed, "I must return home!" He stood up and bowed to the sparrow fairy, thanking her for her hospitality.

The sparrow brought out two boxes, one large and one small. "Please take one as a present," she told the old man. He could not very well refuse, so he took the small box. Then he hurried home.

The old woman was quite cross about her husband's absence. And when he told her about his wonderful day at the sparrow's home, she became even more peeved. "You left me to slave all day by myself," she complained, "while you amused yourself?"

The old man hastily took out the small box. "Look at the gift the sparrow gave me!" And he told his wife about the two chests the bird had offered him. The old woman quickly opened the box, and to their astonishment, gold coins spilled out.

"What a wonderful present!" the old man exclaimed.

"How much more money would have been in the larger box!" the old woman complained. And all that night, she could only think about the bigger chest of gold.

The next morning, the old wife asked her husband how he had reached the sparrow's home. "Don't go there!" he warned her. "Remember you cut off her tongue!" But the old woman ignored her husband, thinking only of gold, and she made her way quickly to the sparrow's home. The sparrow was astonished to see the old woman, and all her family wanted to punish the cruel wife. But the sparrow fairy was kind and welcomed the old woman politely.

"My husband sent me for the large box he left behind," the old wife explained. So the sparrow fairy brought out the chest and gave it to the old woman. She quickly hoisted the box on her back and left. The chest was extremely heavy, and the old woman struggled more and more as she walked through the woods. But the thought of the great treasure on her back kept her moving. Finally she paused to rest, and decided to open the box. She untied the cords and peeked inside.

Instantly, a host of demons leaped out. They jumped upon the old woman and beat her relentlessly. She shrieked, and ran away as fast as she could, but the monsters pursued her, nipping at her heels, and tearing her clothes. She fled from the forest, and still the goblins attacked her. Then in the distance, she saw her husband working in the fields, and she ran up to him and hid behind him.

19

"Protect me!" she implored. "The sparrow is trying to kill me!" she cried out. "Such a cruel and wicked bird!"

"No," the old man scolded his wife. "I told you not to go to her!" The monsters circled warily around the old man and his wife. "You are the wicked one, and that is why the demons attack you!" he said in exasperation.

The old woman said nothing. She only trembled and clutched at her husband's legs until the demons finally returned to the forest. But from that day on, the old woman changed her ways. She did not complain about anything nor did she lose her temper. And she stopped yelling at the village children. With each passing day, she became kinder and more gracious. And so she and her husband lived in happiness for the rest of their days, treasuring their gifts from the sparrow fairy—gold from the small box, and wisdom from the large.

Summarized from "The Tongue-cut Sparrow" in Y. T. Ozaki, The Japanese Fairy Book *(Tokyo: Tuttle, 1970)* and Y. Yasuda, Old Tales of Japan *(Tokyo: Tuttle, 1965)*.

Reflections: Self-Confrontation

This elder tale is astonishing. It begins with a nasty old woman, as do many fairy tales, but then the old woman reforms and becomes kind and loving. As we shall see, this is a common theme in elder tales. The lesson from this story might seem obvious: we should admit our faults and change our ways. But if we settled for this moral we would miss the deeper wisdom in elder tales. Ironically, these stories are too realistic about human nature to preach—they offer insight instead.

The wisdom of this story emerges only when compared to tales of youth. There wicked people do not reform, and are summarily punished. In "Snow White," for instance, the evil stepmother is killed at the end, and Cinderella's cruel stepsisters have their eyes gouged out by doves. (This is the original conclusion to the Grimms' story, although later versions were bowdlerized.) Indeed, very few tales of youth depict a wicked person changing. Self-reformation appears mainly in elder tales, and even then the person who repents is an older adult, not a young one.

This feature of elder tales suggests that self-reformation is a task for the second half of life, not the first, a point that Carl Jung emphasized.[1] In his work with older adults, Jung observed that they wrestle with the dark and ugly aspects of their personalities—anger, greed, and cruelty for example. He christened this unsavory side of human nature the *shadow*,[2] and argued that confronting it is a major task of maturity. "The Sparrow's Gift" illustrates this point nicely by personifying the old woman's vices in the form of demons which she must face.

Many other psychologists have independently observed the same thing. From mid-life onward, adults grapple with inner evil and the tragic dimension of life, a process which is particularly clear in artists and writers.[3] The novelist Joseph Conrad, for instance, struggled with despair, hatred, and rage as he moved into the second half of life. His personal ordeal inspired him to start writing for the first time, and the depth of his struggle is reflected in his masterpiece, *The Heart of Darkness*.[4]

Because most people would agree that acknowledging faults is a virtue at any time of life, why would it be particularly important after mid-life? The story offers several important answers, symbolized in small details.

The old woman is bitter and angry, presumably about her poverty and age. Instead of dealing with her frustration directly, though, she takes it out on the sparrow, complaining about how noisy and greedy the bird is. In fact, of course, the old woman is noisy and greedy, not the sparrow. So the old woman blames her own vices on the sparrow, projecting her faults onto the bird. In other fairy tales, the target of this projection is often the spouse, and the wicked old person attacks his or her mate for imagined slights and vices—something quite common in real life marriages, too.

Blaming others unfairly surely seems to be a vice, but it is not always so. Sometimes projection is psychologically useful, and this is especially true in adolescence. Plagued by self-doubts, teenagers typically worry about real and imaginary shortcomings, and

21

dwelling on them can paralyze a young person, preventing him or her from getting on with life. By blaming other people for their problems, adolescents can marshal their uncertain reserves of self-confidence.[5] Not surprisingly, then, projection is the rule in tales of youth. In a typical story, a young woman may murder her suitors, or a young man may look like a savage beast. These youths either do evil or look evil, but the story excuses them and blames their misdeeds on the real villain—usually a wicked old witch, or an evil old tyrant who casts a spell on the innocent youth. The young victim then sets out to overthrow the villain, and the same often occurs in real life: adolescents make parents and teachers out to be wicked monsters and defy them.

If projection is often normal and helpful in youth, "The Sparrow's Gift" warns us that the practice must cease in the second half of life. And this, indeed, is a major task for maturity, as Jung and other psychotherapists have argued. Confirmation of the point comes from systematic research in adult development. For instance, one team of investigators studied 268 men from the time they were students at Harvard University in the early 1940's until the present.[6] Another research group, starting in the 1920's, observed 248 individuals from infancy, and another 212 from fifth grade, continuing their work to the present.[7] Among the wealth of information gathered by these researchers, several findings are relevant to "The Sparrow's Gift." The researchers found that individuals tended to use projection frequently in youth, but they stopped as they matured. More importantly, those people who failed to develop in adulthood and who suffered from psychological difficulties—ranging from alcoholism to chronic depression—continued to use projection heavily. Conversely, self-confrontation, and self-responsibility correlated with health and happiness. As "The Sparrow's Gift" puts it, facing the demons inside is a prerequisite to successful aging.

A case from my psychotherapeutic practice emphasizes the point, with a dramatic parallel to the story. Mr. L came to therapy in his early 50's for a vague sense of depression and uneasiness, which he attributed to difficulties at work. He had been dissatisfied with his job for some years, as are many men at mid-life, and blamed his problems on a younger colleague. As Mr. L reviewed the events of his life and career, he began to realize that similar problems had cropped up repeatedly at work and at home—too many to blame on other people. About a year into therapy, the insight blossomed when Mr. L declared in one session, "Now I know why I get so mad at my colleague! He acts exactly the way I used to when I was in my 20's—self-righteous and stubborn!" The insight was a turning point for Mr. L and he made a concerted effort to stop offering his opinions to everybody on everything. The turmoil at work and at home subsided, and Mr. L soon embarked upon a fruitful and creative new phase in his career.

Figuratively speaking, Mr. L acknowledged the demons in his own heart and reformed, just like the old woman in "The Sparrow's Gift."[8] And cases from psychotherapy are often dramatically similar to fairy tales because they both compress important developmental tasks into a short period of time, like time-lapse photography. With elder tales, the condensation is for dramatic effect, and with psychotherapy, by conscious design.

The present story contains another insightful detail about the psychology of maturity. In becoming aware of her own faults, the old woman brings to consciousness what was unconscious before. This process of evolving awareness illuminates the deeper symbolism of the location of the drama at the edge of a forest.

As psychoanalysts have noted, forests often appear in dreams and fairy tales as a symbol of the unconscious: forests are dark, unknown places, filled with frightening creatures, just as the unconscious seems dark, unknown, and filled with uncivilized and unacceptable impulses. By having the old woman live at the edge of the forest and go freely into the wilderness, our story suggests that she lives at the edge of the unconscious, and that one of her tasks is to confront those issues and make them conscious. Nor is the liminal location unique to this story. In "Fortune and the Woodcutter," the old man also lives on the edge of the forest, and so do many other protagonists in elder tales, as we shall see.

In fact, adults do become more open to the unconscious with greater psychological maturity. In the longitudinal research mentioned before, for instance, many individuals did not remember real childhood traumas, such as a mother's suicide, when they were asked about them in adolescence—presumably because the events were too difficult to deal with. (The researchers, of course, knew about the traumatic events.) From middle age onward, the same individuals regained their recollections of trauma, and were able to come to terms with them, as they mastered the conflicts they could not tolerate before.[9] Clinicians working with older adults have also commented on the phenomenon.[10] Mature individuals are more capable of dealing with unpleasant or conflictual issues and so have less need to repress them. As one gentleman in therapy put it, "When I was 20, I hated my father! I couldn't bear to even think about him. Now that I am 75, what does it matter? And ironically, I see how much I am like him!"

The self-confrontation portrayed in "The Sparrow's Gift" is so dramatic that it may seem magical and unbelievable. The latter is not true, as systematic research and clinical experience shows, but the former is. Indeed, self-reformation comprises a vital form in which magic returns in the second half of life.

4

The Magic Towel

(from Japan)

Once upon a time, an old woman lived with her son and daughter-in-law. The old mother resented the young woman's beauty and made life hard for her, ordering her to do all the heavy work in the house. The young woman was sweet and kind, and made no complaint, which only infuriated the old woman more.

One day the old woman told her daughter-in-law to make rice cakes, and when the young woman was finished, the old mother counted them. Then she went to the village on an errand. A travelling monk stopped by at the house, and the young woman gave him a rice cake out of kindness. After the priest left, the old mother returned, counted the cakes, and immediately noticed one was missing.

"What have you done with the last cake!" she shrieked at her daughter-in-law, "you vain, greedy thing!"

"I gave it to a monk," the young woman explained, trying to calm the old woman.

"Well you must fetch it back!" the mother-in-law yelled. So the young wife ran after the monk, apologized profusely, and asked for the rice cake back.

The monk laughed, and returned the gift. Then he gave the young woman a small towel. "Use it to wash your face," he said. "I know that life is hard with your mother-in-law."

From then on, the old mother noticed that her daughter-in-law became more and more beautiful. This made the old woman ever more jealous, and so she spied on her daughter-in-law one morning. She saw the young woman wipe her face with the towel, and each time she did so, her face became more radiant and lovely. "She uses a magic towel!" the old woman muttered to herself. So the next day, the old woman sent her daughter-in-law on an errand, and then stole the magic towel. She washed her face and peered at herself in the mirror. But she saw no change. "I am older," the mother-in-law thought, "so I must wash harder!" She wiped her face over and over, and then looked in the mirror. To her horror, her face became long and horse-like, and then hairy and round like a monkey's. Finally her features changed into a goblin's!

"Aie!" the old woman cried and collapsed on the floor. At that moment, her daughter-in-law returned. She saw the demon in the house and turned to flee. The old woman cried out, "Help me!"

The daughter-in-law recognized the old woman's voice and felt sorry for her. "You must find a remedy!" the old woman pleaded. So the daughter-in-law ran out, looking for the monk.

She found him some distance away and told him what happened. He laughed. "When a wicked person uses the towel," the monk said, "they end up looking like a demon!"

"Is there no cure?" the young woman asked.

"Yes," the monk laughed again, "just tell your mother-in-law to use the other side of the towel!"

The young wife ran home and told the old woman the remedy. The mother-in-law immediately turned the towel over and wiped her face. The first time she did so, her face changed from a goblin's to a monkey's. The second time, it turned into a horse's snout, and the third time, it became her own wrinkled but human face.

The old woman embraced her daughter-in-law and wept.

"Dear daughter," the old mother begged for forgiveness, "I did not see how ugly I was toward you!" And from that day on, the old mother never spoke a cross word to anyone. She became kind and generous, and worked side by side with her daughter-in-law. The old mother hoped that the priest with the magic towel would return some day, so she could thank him. But he never came back—nor did he need to.

Summarized from "The Priest's Towel" in R. Dorson, Folk Legends of Japan *(Tokyo: Tuttle, 1962). A similar tale can be found in F. H. Mayer,* Ancient Tales in Modern Japan *(Bloomington, Ind.: Indiana University Press, 1985).*

Reflections: Mask and Self

"The Magic Towel" reiterates the drama of self-reformation we saw in "The Sparrow's Gift." But the present story adds several perceptive new insights which show why self-reformation is a task for the second half of life.

Consider the power of the magic towel. It makes the kind young woman ever more beautiful, and the jealous old woman ever more hideous. The towel wipes away outward appearances, and reveals the face of the soul. It removes masks, and this highlights an important difference between the psychology of youth and maturity.

Most social situations require masks of various kinds—a happy one at cocktail parties, or an industrious one at work, for instance. Indeed, in many social and professional circles, "image" can be as significant as substance, and the mask can be more important than the person. Masks are an integral part of modern life, partly because individuals must play so many different roles— parent, spouse, worker, friend, citizen, to name just a few. (This is especially true of women, not because of the traditional feminine emphasis on appearances, but because women typically play more roles than men.) With each role come certain conventional behaviors, and these shape the social masks individuals wear.

Jung called these social appearances the *persona,* from the Greek term for the masks which ancient actors wore to identify their particular roles in a play.[1] Developing this *persona,* he argued, is a major task of growing up, and other psychologists concur that learning complex social roles and mastering the masks that go with them is a vital challenge for youth. To be sure, most people decry two-faced or "phony" individuals, but usually only when someone uses masks excessively, or deceptively.

If youth must master the art of wearing masks, "The Magic Towel" suggests that adults must learn to remove them, and attend to inner substance rather than outward appearances. To dramatize the point, we can compare "The Magic Towel" to Oscar Wilde's modern fairy tale, *Portrait of Dorian Gray.* In Wilde's novel, Dorian Gray remains young and handsome over the years through the work of a powerful magic spell. At the same time, a secret portrait of him becomes progressively more hideous, reflecting the corruption of his soul. Ultimately, Dorian perishes. His magic operates in a way opposite to that of the magic towel's, with correspondingly opposed results. (Interestingly, many painters like Rembrandt, Titian, Hals, and Goya, focus on capturing outward appearances in their early work, but shift later in life to an emphasis on the psychological or spiritual substance of their subjects, seeking to portray inner nature, rather than outer appearance.[2])

"The Magic Towel" provides other symbolic details about self-confrontation. First, the old mother-in-law changes her ways only when she is confronted with a horrifying supernatural event—becoming a demon. A similar terrifying event happens in "The Sparrow's Gift," and the meaning is not hard to understand. Extraordinary events are often necessary to force self-confrontation and growth, and sometimes only tragedy—the death of a child, a traumatic divorce, or failing in a job—works.

Notice, too, that the story begins by contrasting the nasty old woman with her kind, patient daughter-in-law. One is bad, the other good, and the distinction between the two is clear-cut. At the end of the story, however, the stark contrast is blurred. The old woman recognizes her evil, and resolves to reform; she accepts both her good and evil sides. This movement away from a stark dualism also occurs in "The Sparrow's Gift" and symbolizes an important shift from youthful reasoning to mature thinking.

Youthful logic typically involves either/or categories, in which everything is classified as black or white. For instance, young children, unable to think in more sophisticated ways, divide the world into the two mutually exclusive camps of "good" and "bad."[3] Adolescents also use an either/or kind of thinking, but in a different way. They are capable of making much more sophisticated judgments, but they also gravitate toward abstract ideals,[4] and their idealism easily becomes extreme. People are therefore considered to be either superlatively "good" or superlatively "bad."

Experience forces adults to abandon this dichotomous thinking, and by mid-life, most people learn many shades of grey.[5] If adolescents typically assume that there are right and wrong answers, young adults shift to a more relativistic viewpoint, accepting many "right" answers. With further experience, adults emphasize practical compromises even more, and accept the many extenuating circumstances which occur in everyday life. Tolerance of one's own faults and those of others, as well as a greater acceptance of ambiguity and uncertainty is the result. Unlike the youth, the mature adult can hold many conflicting positions in mind at the same time, without having to simplify matters. But this is not merely an intellectual development. Emotional growth is required—the ability to tolerate the anxiety of uncertainty, for instance, and to surrender, however painfully, youthful dreams of perfection.[6]

Although "The Magic Towel" and "The Sparrow's Gift" both come from Japan, other elder tales from around the world exhibit the same themes of self-confrontation and self-reformation.[7] In the Russian story of "Jack Frost,"[8] for instance, a wicked old stepmother persecutes her stepdaughter, while pampering her own grown children. But the stepmother's greed leads to the death of her two daughters. Devastated by the tragedy, the stepmother realizes how cruel and proud she has been. She repents and reforms her ways. (This is essentially the Cinderella story, in the form of an elder tale, and told more from the stepmother's viewpoint.)

In a similar vein, the Jewish tale of "The Miser"[9] tells the story of a man who hoards his money and begrudges anyone the slightest charity. One day he accidentally falls into the hands of demons who intend to kill him. The old miser just barely escapes, and the terror of his experience prompts him to reform his ways, making him generous and kind. Charles Dickens' classic tale, *A Christmas Carol,* I should add, offers a perfect example of the self-reformation theme, although it is technically not an elder tale, since it was written by one person. In Dickens' tale, the old miser Scrooge is visited by the spirits of Christmas past, present, and future. The last is the horrifying apparition that prompts him to reform.

From around the world, elder tales bring the same message: confronting one's own evil is a major task of maturity. And far from being too rigid to change, the older adults in elder tales are the ones who confront themselves. Self-reformation is a task—and virtue—of the second half of life.

5

The Old Alchemist

(from Burma)

nce upon a time, there lived an old man with his beautiful daughter. She fell in love with a handsome lad, and the two married with the old man's blessing. The young couple led a happy life, except for one problem: the husband spent his time working on alchemy, dreaming of a way to turn base elements into gold. Soon enough, he ran through his patrimony, and the young wife struggled to buy food each day. She finally asked her husband to find a job, but he protested. "I am on the verge of a breakthrough!" he insisted. "When I succeed, we will be rich beyond our dreams!"

Finally the young wife told her father about the problem. He was surprised to learn that his son-in-law was an alchemist, but he promised to help his daughter and asked to see him the next day. The young man went reluctantly, expecting a reprimand. To his surprise, his father-in-law confided in him, "I, too, was an alchemist when I was young!" The father-in-law inquired about the young man's work, and the two spent the afternoon talking. Finally the old man stirred with excitement. "You have done everything I did!" he exclaimed. "You are surely on the verge of a breakthrough. But you need one more ingredient to change base elements into gold, and I have only recently discovered this secret." The old man paused and sighed. "But I am too old to undertake the task. It requires much work."

"I can do it, dear father!" the young man volunteered. The old man brightened. "Yes, perhaps you can." Then he leaned over and whispered, "The ingredient you need is the silver powder that grows on banana leaves. This powder becomes magic when you plant the bananas yourself, and cast certain spells upon it."

"How much powder do we need?" the young man asked. "Two pounds," the old man replied.

The son-in-law thought out loud, "That requires hundreds of banana plants!"

"Yes," the old man sighed, "and that is why I cannot complete the work myself." "Do not fear!" the young man said, "I will!" And so the old man taught his son-in-law the incantations and loaned him money for the project.

The next day, the young man bought some land, and cleared it. He dug the ground himself, just as the old man had instructed him, planted the bananas, and murmured the magic spells over them. Each day he examined his plants, keeping weeds and pests away, and when the plants bore fruit, he collected the silver powder from the leaves. There was scarcely any on each plant, and so the young man bought more land, and cultivated more bananas. After several years, the young man collected two pounds of the magic dust. He rushed to his father-in-law's house.

"I have the magic powder!" the young man exclaimed. "Wonderful!" the old man rejoiced. "Now I can show you how to turn base elements into gold! But first you must bring your wife here. We need her help." The young man was puzzled, but obeyed. When she appeared, the old man asked his daughter, "While your husband was collecting the banana powder, what did you do with the fruits?"

"Why I sold them," the daughter said, "and that is how we earned a living."

"Did you save any money?" the father asked.

"Yes," she replied.

"May I see it?" the old man asked. So his daughter hurried home and returned with several bags. The old man opened them, saw they were full of gold, and poured the coins on the floor. Then he took a handful of dirt, and put it next to the gold.

"See," he turned to his son-in-law, "you have changed base elements into gold!"

For a tense moment, the young man was silent. Then he laughed, seeing the wisdom in the old man's trick. And from that day on, the young man and his wife prospered greatly. He tended the plants while she went to the market, selling the bananas. And they both honored the old man as the wisest of alchemists.

Summarized from "Use a Thorn to Draw a Thorn," in E. Brockett, Burmese and Thai Fairy Tales *(London: Frederick Muller, 1965).*

Reflections: Wisdom

Wisdom, tradition says, is a virtue of age. Somewhat surprisingly, psychology has only recently begun to examine the nature of this virtue,[1] possibly because gerontology has previously been occupied with studying the deficits of aging, and not the developments of maturity. "The Wise Alchemist" and similar elder tales are thus invaluable in sketching out a picture of wisdom, and they portray an important developmental task for the second half of life.

The present story begins with circumstances that may be uncomfortably familiar to parents of grown children. The old man seems to be in a no-win situation with his son-in-law. If he tries to intervene in the family problem, he risks alienating the young man. But if he does nothing, his daughter and any future grandchildren face poverty. Caught in this dilemma, the old father comes up with a clever—and wise—solution. So our story outlines the first feature of wisdom: it is *practical*. Wisdom is not sublime metaphysical knowledge, but a skill that helps solve real human problems.

This theme recurs in other elder tales and fits well with recent findings in cognitive psychology. Older adults excel at practical problem-solving, particularly dealing with complex everyday difficulties. They do less well on traditional measures of abstract reasoning compared to college students. Although this difference was usually explained as a deficit—the intellectual deterioration due to age—more recent work suggests that mature individuals consciously reject abstract reasoning as irrelevant to real-life problems.[2] Their wisdom involves practical reason; the intelligence of youth relies more on "pure" reason.

In the story, the old father's wisdom depends on indirect action. He does not simply command the young man to abandon alchemy and find a practical job. This may seem to be common sense—never tell in-laws what to do—but the old man's discretion is significant because the story comes from Burma. There elders enjoy a great deal of social authority, so in real life the old man could just order the young man to change his ways.

The old father's solution involves deliberate deceit. This is surprising, since we usually associate wisdom with virtue, not mendacity, but the theme can be seen in many other elder tales, like the Gypsy story of "The Deluded Dragon," the Chinese tale of "The Groom's Crimes," and the Cossack story, "The Ungrateful Children."[3] Wisdom, elder tales suggest, involves an older person deceiving a younger one.

Deceit, of course, is the talent of "con artists." What distinguishes the old alchemist from a con man is integrity. The old father does not seek his own gain but rather the good of the young man's family, and of course, the old man's daughter. The father's motivation is altruistic. This is crucial to the concept of wisdom, and the unsavory alternative is frequently portrayed in youth tales. There, the young protagonist typically contends with a selfish old person, who tries to trick the youth out of a treasure. The young protagonist falls for the trick until somebody tells him or her about the deception. The helpful person is usually an old man or woman, but an *unselfish* one—the wise old man or the good witch. The old alchemist is just such a benevolent figure. Although the present story does not go into the matter, we can conjecture that the old father has mastered both his greed and his pride. He does not try to dominate the young man simply to satisfy his own ego, nor does he seek to make money for himself. (Indeed, he loans his money to the youth.)

Notice that the old man's deception works because it depends on a keen understanding of human psychology—particularly that of youth. The old man does not belittle the young man's dream of turning base elements into gold, nor does he forbid the enterprise. He seems to understand that dreams are the lifeblood of youth, whether the aspirations involve social reform, fame, universal truth, or changing base elements into gold. Take away those ambitions and youth is left with few alternatives—rebellion or apathy. Validate those dreams, as the old man does, and youth will endure almost any drudgery or risk. So the old father wisely *diverts* rather than *obstructs* the young man's enthusiasm. He harnesses the young man's ambition, and this is true alchemy, transmuting youthful idealism into mature pragmatism.

A small detail in the story offers a related insight about wisdom. The young man fiddles with chemicals, while the old father ponders the psychology of youth. In general, tales of youth focus on *magic objects,* while elder tales emphasize *psychological insights.* For instance, in an escapade common to youth tales around the world, the young hero rescues the heroine from an evil witch (or the heroine rescues the hero, although this is less common). As the witch pursues them, the hero or heroine throws down a comb, which becomes a forest that blocks the witch. When the witch breaks through and starts to catch up with the young couple, they throw down something else—like a scarf—which becomes a mountain. This goes on for a while, with a variety of objects, until the young hero and heroine escape. The magic objects vary from story to story, and country to country, but the reliance on them does not. The old alchemist, by contrast, uses objects only as a ruse—like the banana powder. He relies upon insights into human nature, not magic. Indeed, because there is no magic in the "The Old Alchemist," the story may not seem like a true fairy tale. But the point of elder tales is that magic plays a different role in later life than in youth. It does not *solve* the problems of life, but rather *enriches* experience.

This divergence between elder stories and tales of youth

35

reflects an important difference between the psychology of the first and second halves of life. Youth gravitates towards objects and tries to solve human problems with *things.* Young men, for instance, stereotypically lavish their attention on cars and motorcycles, and this fascination serves important psychological functions. Powerful engines can alleviate self-doubt, and shiny cars impress dates. Similarly, young women traditionally focus on clothes and jewelry, using ornaments to bolster their self-esteem, ensure popularity, and attract boyfriends. These stereotypical roles change today, of course, and young men may wear more jewelry than young women, but the adolescent preoccupation with objects remains.

With experience, mature adults turn to an understanding of human nature rather than new gadgets—relying on psychology rather than technology.[4] As the statesman Adlai Stevenson once said about the mature adult: "The knowledge he has acquired with age is not a knowledge of formulas or forms of words, but of people, places, and actions . . . the human experiences and emotions of this world, and of oneself and other men."[5] The alternative to wisdom is often a fixation on objects, ultimately leading to hoarding possessions—the stereotype of the old miser. If preoccupation with and cleverness about things is a virtue of young adults, wisdom and insight into human nature is a task for maturity.

The career of a Mr. D, whom I interviewed in a study on adult cognition, illustrates the point. He started out as an engineer for a large company, and spent his time working out technical details in various projects. Over the years, he rose through the ranks of the company until he became its president in his early 60's, overseeing a multi-billion dollar operation. Although he still identified himself as "basically an engineer at heart," Mr. D refrained from commenting on technical projects. He focused instead on being a good judge of people. "I can't follow the technical details any more," he explained, "but I'm pretty good at judging who to trust when they recommend a project, and who not to trust. That's my responsibility now, figuring people out, not projects." His experience provides reassuring advice for an increasingly technological society: young adults may master new gadgets more quickly—

from computers to genetic engineering—but the ability to deal effectively with interpersonal problems remains invaluable. That capacity is wisdom. And as we shall see in the next tale, wisdom is a developmental task requiring self-confrontation and reflection.

6

The Wise Merchant

(a Jewish tale)

nce upon a time, a merchant and his grown son set out on a sea voyage. They carried a chest full of jewels to sell on the journey, but told no one about their fortune. One day, the merchant overheard the sailors whispering among themselves. They had discovered his treasure and were plotting to kill him and his son to steal the jewels!

The merchant was beside himself with fear, and he paced back and forth in his cabin, trying to figure a way out of the predicament. His son asked what was the matter, and his father told him.

"We must fight them!" the young man declared.

"No," the old man replied, "they will overpower us!"

Sometime later, the merchant stormed out on the deck. "You fool of a son!" he cried out, "you never heed my advice!"

"Old man!" the son yelled back, "you have nothing to say worth hearing!"

The sailors gathered round curiously as father and son started cursing at each other. Then the old man rushed to his cabin, and dragged out his chest of jewels. "Ungrateful son!" the merchant shrieked. "I would rather die in poverty than have you inherit my wealth!" With that, the merchant opened his treasure chest and the sailors gasped at the sight of all the jewels. Then the merchant rushed to the railing and before anyone could stop him, he threw his treasure overboard.

In the next moment, father and son stared at the empty box, and then they collapsed upon each other, weeping over what they had done. Later, when they were alone in their cabin, the father said, "We had to do it, son. There was no other way to save our lives!"

"Yes," the son replied, "your plan was the best."

The ship soon docked, and the merchant and his son hurried to the magistrate of the city. They charged the sailors with piracy and attempted murder, and the magistrate arrested the sailors. The judge asked the sailors if they had seen the old man throw his treasure overboard, and they agreed. So he convicted them all. "What man would throw away his life's savings, except if he feared for his life?" the judge asked. The pirates offered to replace the merchant's jewels, and in return for that the judge spared their lives.

Summarized from "The Wise Merchant," in G. Friedlander, The Jewish Fairy Book *(New York: Stokes, 1920).*

Reflections: Wisdom and Evil

This elder tale reiterates the portrait of wisdom we saw in "The Old Alchemist." The merchant uses a clever deception to solve a very practical and dangerous problem. But the tale adds two new points which hint at how wisdom develops psychologically in the second half of life.

First of all, the merchant's wisdom depends on his knowledge of human evil, and particularly what men will do out of greed. When he overhears the sailors plotting to murder him to steal his treasure, the merchant does not naively try to bargain with the pirates, offering them his jewels in return for his life. Although it is not explicitly mentioned in the tale, one can infer that the merchant realizes his danger: even if he gave the sailors his fortune, they would still have to kill him to keep their robbery secret.

Simply knowing about human evil, however, is not sufficient for wisdom. The old merchant has to go one step further and master his own covetousness. Only then can he throw away his life's savings. Indeed, this is precisely why the old man's ruse works: the pirates are so greedy, they cannot imagine that anybody would willingly throw away a king's ransom. So they never suspect that the merchant knows about their plot. Avarice makes the pirates vulnerable to the old man's deception. The story does not go into detail about how the merchant conquers his greed, but we have already met the theme in "The Sparrow's Gift" and "The Magic Towel." Presumably, the merchant has faced the *shadow* in his own soul, and come to terms with it. And other fairy tales are clear about what happens if an older person does not do so. In the tale of "The Wizard King,"[1] for instance, an old king's greed kills him at the end. And in the familiar story of "Rumpelstiltskin," the old dwarf's rage proves to be his own undoing.

The view that wisdom involves knowledge of human evil is immortalized in the well-known phrase, "sadder but wiser"—after being used or abused by others, we learn the darker side of human nature. And it is not hard to see why mastery of one's *own* evil is a prerequisite of wisdom. As long as an individual cannot control his own impulses, he is a slave to them, and so easily duped. Con men, after all, typically lure their victims by promising ways to get rich quickly. Greed is their best accomplice.

Wisdom as mastery of human evil appears in other elder tales. In the Gypsy story of "The Deluded Dragon,"[2] for instance, an old man awakens at night while on a journey and overhears two dragons plotting to kill him. Forewarned about this heinous scheme, but lacking the strength to fight the beasts, he bluffs them in a clever deception and escapes with their treasure. Dragons are typically symbols of evil in Western folklore, so this elder tale nicely illustrates how wisdom involves an encounter with, and insight into, evil. Since dragons are usually killed by a hero in tales of youth, the present elder tale also contrasts heroism with wisdom— the difference between battle and guile.

In the Cossack tale of "The Ungrateful Children,"[3] the connection between evil and wisdom is even more explicit. Here, as in

41

Shakespeare's *King Lear,* an old man divides his estate among his grown children and then goes to live with them, naively thinking that he will spend the rest of his days in comfort. But his children soon put him out. Unlike the case of Lear, however, a mysterious stranger appears and helps the old man trick his children into taking him back again. The old father pretends he has a great treasure hidden away, and so his children fawn over him in order to inherit the wealth. In this tale, the helpful stranger is a shadowy figure whose identity is unclear, but he appears to be the Devil himself.[4] Taken together, elder tales portray wisdom as the result not just of long experience with people, but more importantly, of self-exploration. Wisdom develops from self-confrontation and self-mastery.

Another new element in "The Wise Merchant" is the fact that the old merchant is attacked by *younger* men. The theme resurfaces in many other elder tales. And when, for example, the older person's own children plot to steal from him, as in "The Ungrateful Children," the situation can be quite dramatic. This brings us to an important motif in elder tales: the war between the generations, portrayed so dramatically in mythology. The Greek god Zeus, for instance, overthrew his father and seized control of Olympus. But Zeus remained frightened of a younger god who would overthrow him in his turn. In a more celebrated mythological example, young Oedipus slew his father, King Laius, and took his father's throne, albeit unknowingly. Oedipus thus fulfilled the prophecy that had compelled Laius to abandon Oedipus as an infant in the wilderness.

The archetypal conflict between generations occurs in many forms in real life. In the workplace, for example, older workers must often compete with younger ones, and fear losing their jobs. Senior executives start watching out for ambitious junior colleagues eager to unseat them. Ironically, if the rallying cry of youth is "Don't trust anyone over 30," the hidden anxiety of maturity is "Don't trust anyone under 30!"

The present elder tale suggests that wisdom can help the older adult cope with competition from youth—through clever deception. If age robs an individual of physical strength, speed, and stamina, wisdom more than compensates. However, the basic conflict remains, and a more lasting resolution to the clash between generations requires something beyond wisdom. That further development is the subject of the next story.

7

The Magic Forest

(a Croatian tale)

 ong ago, an old woman lived with her son on the edge of an enchanted forest. One spring day, the young man wandered into the woods, and sat upon a tree stump. A beautiful silver snake crawled out from the roots and the young man exclaimed, "What a lovely snake! I should like to take it home for a pet!"

In the next moment, the snake changed into a fair maiden, with golden hair and a pretty dress. "You have freed me from a dreadful spell!" the maiden said, but she was careful not to open her mouth too far. She was really a snake taking on a human form through magic, and her tongue was still forked.

All that day, the young man wandered with her in the enchanted forest, and by evening, he proposed they marry. She consented, and so he took the maiden home with him. "This is my wife-to-be," the son told his mother.

The mother felt happy for her son, until she took one look at the beautiful maiden. The old woman was wise in the ways of this world and the next, and she felt suspicious. "Beware, my son," she warned him. "I fear this woman is a snake and that she has a forked tongue in her mouth."

Her son was outraged. "You are a witch!" he cried out to his mother, and turned against her from that day.

The young man married, and moved his new wife in with him and his mother. The beautiful woman made life hard for the old mother, and forced her do all the chores. One day, the wife turned to the old woman, and an evil light burned in her lovely eyes. "Go to the top of a mountain," the wife told the old mother, "and fetch me some snow. I want to wash my face in it, to keep my beauty."

"I will fall to my death on the mountain!" the old woman protested.

"All the better!" the wife replied.

The old woman dared not argue further, because she feared her son would back his wife. So she struggled up the steep and rocky mountain paths, and there, high beneath the heavens, the old mother paused to pray for help. But then she stopped herself. "If I pray," she thought, "God will know my son's sins." And so the old mother kept silent. But more than prayers reach the ears of heaven, and the old woman returned home safely, carrying a pail of snow.

Later, in the middle of winter, the young wife craved a fresh fish. "Go to the lake," she ordered the old mother, "and fetch me a fish!"

"The ice will break beneath me," the old woman protested, "and I shall drown!"

"All the better!" the wife laughed, with an evil glint in her eyes, and the young man laughed also, to please his wife.

So the old woman struggled through the snow with a heavy heart. When she came to the lake, the ice cracked beneath her feet and she almost fell in the water. She wanted to pray for help, but she dared not. "God will learn of my son's great sin!" she feared. At that moment, a gull flew over the lake, carrying a large fish in its beak. The fish wriggled out of the bird's mouth, and fell right at the old mother's feet. She thanked God for his help, and returned home. The young wife scowled with disappointment.

Some time later, the old woman sat by the fire in the

evening, and picked up her son's shirts to mend. The young wife snatched the clothes away. "You will ruin them!" she shrieked.

"Mind my wife," the son told his mother, and so the old woman went outside, heartbroken. She sat alone on the frozen porch, staring at the snow. Finally she cried out in her pain, "Dear God, help me!"

Moments later, a poor young woman from the village appeared, carrying a load of wood. Her coat was torn and she shivered in the cold. "Do you need kindling?" the girl asked. "I have some to sell."

"No, dear girl," the old mother shook her head. "But come here," she offered, "I will mend your coat for you." And the old woman quickly sewed the coat so that it was just like new.

"Thank you, dear mother," the maiden said, and she gave the old woman a bundle of kindling in gratitude.

That night, the snake woman and the young man went to a dinner in the village. "Have a hot bath ready for me when I return!" the young wife ordered the old mother, "and feed the hens and clean their coop!" The young woman, you see, prided herself on her hens and she planned a party for all the villagers when the eggs hatched. No one else had hens that laid eggs in the middle of winter, but then no one else used magic.

After her son and his wife left, the old woman lit a fire, and went outside to draw water for the bath. All of a sudden, she heard giggling from the house. She rushed back, and to her surprise, she discovered twelve little men, dancing around the kitchen. Their coats were red like fire, their beards were grey like smoke, and their eyes twinkled like bright coals.

"Who are you?" the old woman exclaimed in surprise.

"Fire elves!" the little men replied. Then they started dancing, and drew the old woman into their circle. Soon the old woman clapped her hands and danced with the elves, thanking God for their cheer. She felt young and joyous again, and she recalled how she danced and sang with her husband, long ago. Then she remembered her son, and her heart grew heavy. She sat down, and all the elves gathered round her.

"What is the matter?" asked the tiniest elf, whose name was Wee Tintilinkie. The old woman explained how her son was bewitched by the snake woman, and so all the elves put their heads together and thought and thought. Then Wee Tintilinkie came up with a plan. "We can put magpie eggs in the hen house," he suggested. "Snakes crave magpies," he explained, "so when the chicks hatch, the snake woman will hunger for them. She will stick out her forked tongue and that will expose her!" All the elves clapped their hands, pleased with the plan.

At that moment, the wife returned and the elves leaped into the air, with a flash of smoke. Wee Tintilinkie jumped into the fire.

"What was that?" the wife demanded.

"The draft fanned the fire," the old woman explained.

"What is that?" the suspicious wife asked again, pointing to the fire, where Wee Tintilinkie glowed like a flaming log.

"Just coals in the fire!" the old mother replied. The snake wife looked more closely, and she stuck her nose so near Wee Tintilinkie, he could not resist. He tweaked the wife's nose and she shrieked.

"What was that?" the wife yelled at the old mother.

"Watch out!" The old mother suppressed a laugh. "There are chestnuts in the fire!"

The wife went away mumbling angrily to herself, and Wee Tintilinkie ran out to look for magpies.

The day soon arrived when the young wife invited the village over to admire her newly hatched chicks. She did not bother to check on the birds beforehand, and so the moment she saw the baby magpies, she was overcome with a craving

48

for them. She stuck out her forked tongue, fell to the floor, and slithered toward the chicks. Everybody screamed and fled. Mothers dragged their children away, and fathers crossed themselves.

The old mother turned sadly to her son. "Now you have seen what your wife really is!" But the young man was enraged, still bewitched by his wife.

"You are a witch!" he yelled at his mother, and told her to leave his house and never return.

The old woman was heartbroken, but she had no desire to stay in her own home anymore. She only asked her son to let her depart at night. "Otherwise the villagers will see everything and speak ill of you," she explained.

That night, the old woman left, taking only an old cloak and a small bundle of kindling to keep her warm in the winter. And when she crossed the threshold of her home, the fire went out in the hearth, and the crucifix fell from the wall. In that moment, the son knew what a great sin he had committed, and the snake woman's spells fell away from him. He wanted to run after his mother, but he dared not, fearful now of his wife's magic.

"Let us follow the old woman," he suggested to his wife.

"Yes," the snake woman said. "We can watch her die!"

Far away in the wintry wilderness, the old woman stopped and built a fire to warm herself. When the wood caught fire, the twelve elves appeared again, laughing and singing. But they saw how downhearted the old mother felt, and they sat next to her. "What is wrong?" Wee Tintilinkie asked. The old mother explained what happened, and the elves thought long and hard, pulling on their beards.

"Let us go to the Forest King," Wee Tintilinkie suggested. "He will help us." So one of the elves blew on a small silver horn, and a magnificent stag appeared from the forest. Then another elf blew a horn, and twelve squirrels appeared. The elves put the old mother on the stag, and each one mounted a squirrel. Then they rode off into the forest. Far behind them, the son and the snake wife followed.

At the center of the woods stood an oak tree so large it contained seven golden castles, and a village, too. In the greatest of the castles sat the Forest King, and the elves went up to him and explained the old woman's plight. "Can you help me?" the old woman asked. Outside, the son and his wife crept up to a window and listened.

The Forest King nodded. "Yes, indeed," he replied, and waved his hand, pointing to the village in the tree. "Look!" he said. And to the old woman's surprise, she saw the very village in which she had grown up. Her mother and father stood outside their home, and down the lane walked her husband, just as he looked when he came wooing her, many years ago. "You have only to climb the fence and clap," the Forest King said, "and you can live forever in the happiest time of your life."

The old mother was overjoyed, and she ran to the village. Then she stopped. "But what will happen to my son?" she asked the Forest King.

He laughed. "You will know nothing about him. You will live in the time before he was born."

"But what will become of him?" the old woman asked again.

"Leave his fate to him," the Forest King advised.

Then the old woman turned away from the village. "I cannot accept your offer if it means I will forget my life and my son."

At that moment, the forest shuddered and rang out like a great bell. The ground below opened up, and swallowed the oak tree with its golden castles. The Forest King bowed before the old woman. "You have chosen your own life over the greatest joys of magic, and so the enchantment is broken and the land is freed." Then the Forest King vanished with all the elves. The young wife shrieked, and became a serpent again, wriggling away into a hole in the earth. Only the old mother and her son remained in the woods. The young man fell to his knees before his mother and begged her forgiveness, but she had never turned against him, and so they returned to their home.

When spring came, the son fell in love with the young woman who sold kindling. They married and lived happily with the old mother. And soon the family of three became four and five and six, because the son and wife had their own Wee Tintilinkies. And they were magic enough for the old mother.

Summarized from "Stribor's Forest," in I. Berlic-Mazuranic, Croatian Tales of Long Ago *(London: Allen and Unwin, 1924).*

Reflections: Self-Transcendence

"The Magic Forest" is astonishing. It turns the plot of "Cinderella" and "Sleeping Beauty" upside down, and portrays an *old* woman being persecuted by a young one.[1] This reversal alone would make the story an important one, emphasizing the uniqueness of elder tales. But the story is remarkably rich. In particular, the tale elaborates on the nature of worldly wisdom, and then introduces a new theme. In a sense, the present story takes up where "The Old Merchant" and "The Old Alchemist" leave off, and reveals the developmental task that follows wisdom.

In the tale, the old mother immediately suspects that her son's wife is a snake in disguise. Of course, this is often a mother's response in real life when a child marries, but the theme of the dreadful mother-in-law is not the focus of the story. Instead, the old woman's response illustrates another aspect of wisdom. If "The Old Alchemist" and "The Wise Merchant" illustrated how wisdom involves deceiving others, the present tale underscores the importance of *seeing through deceptions.* The old mother's wisdom also contrasts sharply with her son's bewitchment. Although he knows that his wife was a snake, having seen her change before his very eyes, he refuses to recognize the signifi-

51

cance of that fact. The tale thus dramatizes the power of magic in youth—the spell of dreams and ideals, whether they are about true love, universal truth, or social revolution. No doubt because she has been through her own share of dreams and hopes and has emerged with greater realism, like older adults in real life, the mother does not fall for the snake woman's spells.

Wise though she is, the old mother cannot resolve the conflict between herself and her daughter-in-law—the archetypal battle between the generations. Wisdom is not enough, and the story turns to another developmental task.

The new theme revolves around the old woman's love for her son and the degree to which she puts his welfare above her own. Although persecuted by the young wife, the old woman does not pray for help, fearing that God might then punish her son for his sins. Her self-sacrifice dramatizes a vital development of maturity which the psychoanalyst Erik Erikson called "generativity."[2]

Erikson analyzed the lives of such great men as Martin Luther and Mahatma Gandhi and delineated several issues that he felt adults must resolve as they move through life. The task for mid-life, Erikson concluded, is the development of altruistic concern for other people, especially for those in the next generation. Hence, he called this attitude "generativity."

Caring for one's own children is, of course, the most common example of generativity. But sacrificing oneself for one's children does not necessarily qualify. A mother or father may forgo their own needs for their children's sake, but behind the apparent altruism may lurk such other motives as, for instance, the need to have the child succeed so the parents can be proud. Like the magic snake, altruism can take many forms, including egocentricity in a new guise. Indeed, many parents come to a deeper sense of generativity with their *grand*child, because as grandparents they are less invested in the successes or failures of the child.[3]

Generativity does not therefore lie in merely nurturing others, but in the motivation behind such nurturance. In particular, the ability to transcend one's own needs and desires is pivotal. The importance of such *self-transcendence* is portrayed nicely in the tale. Initially, we cannot be sure if the old woman's concern for her son is for *his* sake, or *hers*. She does not challenge the young wife because she fears her son will side with his wife. The old woman's self-sacrificing attitude may also simply be the traditional role of the "good mother," and she may act out of conformity to convention, rather than genuine generativity. These doubts are quickly dispelled after her son rebukes her for trying to mend his shirts. In that moment, she loses her role as a mother, and her place at home. What she has valued above all and sought to preserve—the loyalty of her son—vanishes. But in the next scene, the old mother reveals her authentic generativity: she mends the coat of the young girl who sells kindling. And most importantly, the old woman continues to care for her son, at great cost to herself.

When the elves leap out of the fire, for instance, they offer the old woman a chance to forget her troubles and enjoy herself. She does so, dancing and singing with them, until she remembers her son. Then she returns to worrying about him. Although she can now escape her problems with the magic elves, she chooses not to. The story underscores the old mother's altruism by repeating her decision more dramatically with the Forest King. He gives her a chance to return to the happiest time in her past, but she declines. She transcends her own sorrow for the sake of her son, dramatizing the nature of generativity.

Erikson felt that if an individual failed to develop generativity, further psychological development would not occur in later life. The adult would stagnate, trapped in personal desires and ambitions. Given the inevitability of personal losses with aging, this egocentrism is self-defeating. Self-transcendence is more than a virtue in the second half of life—it is a necessity. Tales of youth, I might add, usually portray the *lack* of generativity in older adults. In one typical plot, a tyrannical father keeps his young daughter locked up and kills off her suitors, unwilling to let her develop her own life. He thinks only of his pride, or wealth, and not his daughter's needs. Or the wicked stepmother squanders the family's wealth on herself, while her stepchildren starve. She indulges egocentric whims, and the next generation suffers. Elder tales like "The Magic Forest" provide a more balanced view, presenting an older person who successfully masters generativity and self-transcendence.

In the tale, an extraordinary thing happens when the old woman refuses the Forest King's magical offer. All the spells in the woods are broken and the whole land is emancipated from enchantment. The old woman's altruism not only benefits her son, but all of society. The story emphasizes an important point here: generativity goes beyond nurturing one's children and ultimately aims at benefitting society. Teaching students, mentoring a younger colleague, or acting as a foster grandparent are all instances of generativity in which society as a whole is the final beneficiary.[4]

The old mother's self-transcendence contrasts sharply with her daughter-in-law's selfishness. The difference is symbolic. Although portrayed in a distinctly unsavory light, the young wife's self-indulgence reflects the prominence, and normality, of self-seeking in youth. Indeed, in most tales of youth, the protagonist seeks something for himself or herself—a great treasure, for instance, or true love. Kindness and generosity help them obtain this goal, but those virtues are basically just means to victory. With the old mother in this elder tale, altruism is not a means—it is the ultimate end. And this theme will reappear constantly in elder tales.

Youth, of course, is a time of lofty ideals and altruistic causes. But these noble visions have a dual purpose: they involve self-sacrifice at the same time that they help the youth establish a sense of self. In working for the Peace Corps, or for social reformation, for instance, young men and women seek a greater good. But in the process, they prove their mettle to themselves and discover who they are. Their idealism is at once self-sacrificing and self-founding, and youth sees no contradiction between social benefit and personal reward. Maturity ushers in a more sober perspective, with the realization that personal desires often clash with the needs of others, and that there is no easy way to resolve the conflict. Altruism then more clearly requires self-transcendence.

The Viennese psychologist Else Frenkel-Brunswick captured the point quite well. After analyzing the biographies of some thousand eminent individuals, ranging from writers and artists to businessmen and politicians, she noted that "I want" dominates youth, while "I ought" governs maturity. The youthful "I want" can include both the welfare of society and the pursuit of personal gratification—altruistic causes and private desires. Either way, though, the "I" is central. In the second half of life, duty and dedication—to family, community, and society—take precedence.

The "I" becomes less important than the "ought." Self-seeking becomes self-transcendence. "Neurotics," Frenkel-Brunswick added, showed the reverse pattern: troubled youths focus on "I ought" more than "I want," while neurotic older adults pursue "I want" rather than "I ought."[5]

The old mother's self-transcendence is dramatic and heart-warming. But fairy tales reflect real life, and an equally astonishing example of generativity can be found in the life of John D. Rockefeller. In the first half of his life, he established the Standard Oil Company and made it into a gigantic monopoly. His business practices were condemned as brutal and rapacious by his contemporaries. Ambition and personal advancement were his principal concerns, not social welfare, and many people considered Rockefeller a monster. In the second half of his life, however, Rockefeller turned to philanthropy. He helped establish the University of Chicago, founded the Rockefeller University in New York, and set up what has now become the world-renowned Rockefeller Foundation. Advancing social welfare became his avowed aim, in contrast to his earlier private ambitions. In fact, his change was so dramatic many people disbelieved it, but it is a pattern that can be seen in the lives of other prominent individuals. Andrew Carnegie, for example, also devoted the first half of his life to amassing a personal fortune, and then shifted later in life to using his wealth to further social improvement.

Rockefeller and Carnegie, however, only dramatize what most individuals do in real life. A variety of studies, including the longitudinal ones at Harvard and the University of California mentioned earlier demonstrate that increasing maturity correlates with greater altruism.[6] This generosity is expressed in the concrete, practical ways older individuals donate more time and money to community work and charity. More significantly, individuals who score higher on various measures of psychological maturity and well-being are more generous than their troubled or "immature" cohorts. Generativity and mental health go hand in hand.

Actually, self-transcendence in later life takes many unobtrusive forms which might be easily overlooked. Consider several everyday examples. Adolescents and young adults tend to proclaim their opinions in a dogmatic, challenging fashion: "This is right!"

and "That is wrong!" They seek absolute truth and assume they know it, unable to distance themselves from their own convictions. (This is, however, often adaptive for adolescents.) As individuals mature, they are more likely to soften their claims by saying things like "*I think* that is wrong," or "*In my opinion* that is right."[7] Mature adults can distance themselves from their opinions, recognizing that their beliefs are opinions rather than truths. They transcend their personal viewpoints.

Two final details in the story deserve analysis. The old woman must climb a mountain to fetch snow, and then risk her life on a frozen lake to catch a fish. These details hint at two other dimensions of self-transcendence. First, the lake, like the ocean, makes a good symbol of the unconscious, and often plays that role in dreams, as psychoanalysts have pointed out. In having the old woman go to the lake and catch a fish, the story suggests that self-transcendence involves retrieving things from the unconscious.[8] We shall see precisely this point in an upcoming story, "The Dragon King of the Sea." Second, mountain tops are usually regarded as sacred places—Zeus inhabited Mt. Olympus, and Yahweh spoke from Mt. Sinai. So the old woman's journey to the summit suggests a sacred or religious dimension to self-transcendence. And that is the focus of the next story.

8

An Old Mother's Sorrow

(from Germany)

ong ago, an old woman sat alone in the evening. Just that day, her last friend had died, leaving her without kin or confidante, and in her grief she remembered the many misfortunes that had befallen her through the years. First one son, and next the other, died when they were but children. Then her husband passed away—followed by her aunt, a sister, and all her relatives one by one. Now she was alone and poor. In her misery the old mother cursed her fate, and then she became angry at God. "What have I done to deserve this?" she lamented.

The sound of church bells awakened the old woman and she looked up with surprise. "I have slept through the night in my chair!" she exclaimed. Then she hurried to church, as she had every morning of her life. When she arrived at the chapel, she was astonished to find that it was not empty as usual. Many people crowded the pews, and the old mother grew uneasy, recognizing no one from her village. Then she realized that the worshippers were relatives and friends who had died!

At that moment, an aunt came up and told the old mother to look beside the altar. There the old woman saw two young men, one hanging from the gallows, and the other bound to the wheel, both criminals and outlaws.

"They are what your sons would have become," the aunt said, "if the good Lord had not taken them to heaven in their innocence." The old mother was filled with sorrow and gratitude and she hurried home, trembling with wonder. There she fell to her knees and gave thanks to God for the grace she could not see before. On the third day, she died, but her eyes were so peaceful that all her neighbors murmured in wonder when they came to bury her.

Summarized from "The Aged Mother," in J. Grimm, The Complete Grimm's Fairy Tales, trans. M. Hunt. (New York: Pantheon, 1944).

Reflections: Transcendence and God

Although not well known, the story of "An Old Mother's Sorrow" comes from the Grimms' collection—perhaps the most popular of fairy tale books. The present story is one of the few elder tales in the volume, suggesting that the story is unusually significant.

The drama begins with the theme of loss: the old woman mourns the death of her friend and then the deaths of her husband and children years before. In anguish, and anger, she demands of God, "Why do I suffer so?" Like the Biblical Job, the old woman can see neither justice nor fairness in her great suffering. She begins with an egocentric perspective, but one eminently human and understandable.

Through a revelation, she discovers a higher purpose in her children's deaths. The tragedies were actually blessings in disguise—not to herself, but to her children, and not from her viewpoint, but from God's. With this insight, she releases her grief, and transcends her egocentric perspective.

Whatever we may think of this particular story—and theologians may blush over it—it brings up the theme of self-transcendence in a specifically religious form. The old widow puts God's plan above her private sorrow, just as the old mother in "The Magic Forest" put her son's welfare above her own happiness. Both protagonists transcend egocentric concerns, although their endpoints differ—one is religious and the other secular. But the underlying process of self-transcendence is the same.

Religious self-transcendence is a traditional task for later life in many cultures. The present tale comes from Germany, and reflects medieval Christian teachings which emphasized the importance of preparing for death in old age.[1] Even earlier, Jewish tradition made spiritual self-transcendence a focus of the second half of life. Old age was considered a sign of God's blessing, and later life was often likened to the Sabbath, a time for studying the Torah and grasping its deeper wisdom, for seeking God, not the self.[2]

Despite the Judeo-Christian background of "An Old Mother's Sorrow," the story is surprisingly non-denominational. With only slight changes in the external descriptions of the building or the arrangement of the altar, the Christian context of this fairy tale would be undetectable and the drama unaltered. The tale might well occur in a Moslem mosque, or a Hindu temple.

In fact, the link between the second half of life and religious forms of self-transcendence occurs in almost every culture and in every historical epoch.[3] Societies from the !Kung in Africa, to the Micronesians of the Pacific, or the Kirghiz of Afghanistan,[4] expect older people to attend to spiritual development and often attribute magical powers to their elders. The elder is thought to transcend personal, mortal concerns, and link human society with the gods. Elders thus preside at sacred ceremonies, from adolescent circumcision rites to harvest rituals. To be sure, just being old does not confer spiritual status on a person. The individual must also be wise, learned in the lore of his or her people, and able to recite sacred legends. Nor is the association between religious transcendence and later life a "primitive" phenomenon. It can also be seen in Western art, where the typical portrait of God is an old man with a long white beard.

Perhaps the clearest discussion of religious self-transcendence in the second half of life comes from Eastern traditions. A good example can be found in ancient China, where Confucius wrote:

> At 15, I set my heart upon learning.
> At 30, I established myself.
> At 40, I no longer had perplexities.
> At 50, I knew the Mandate of Heaven.
> At 60, I was at ease with whatever I heard.

59

> At 70, I could follow my heart's desire without transgressing the boundaries of right.[5]

The comments Confucius made two millenia ago still apply to human development today. Adolescence, 15 years of age, is a time of learning, whether in school, or on the job in an apprenticeship of some sort. At 30, the individual usually settles down, standing firmly on the ground. Worldly interests replace ideals, and job promotions or family problems take precedence. At 40, individuals become confident of themselves, sure of their direction and the worth of their endeavors, part of the generation in charge of society. The perplexities of adolescence are long behind, as well as the doubts that plague young men and women starting a career or family. And the infirmities of later life are only small clouds on the horizon.

At 50 years of age—and this is the important part as far as our elder tale is concerned—a change occurs. The individual turns to the "biddings of Heaven," which Confucius regarded as a divine summons, calling the individual to spiritual pursuits. The mature adult ideally transcends personal and secular endeavors. In subsequent years, the challenge is to deepen the understanding of "Heaven's bidding." By 60, Confucius felt, the individual comes to accept divine dictates, and by 70, the person becomes one with the biddings of heaven, no longer split between private ambitions and heaven's calling. The individual transcends the self.

Confucius was not alone in making religious transcendence a task of later life. In ancient India the great sage Manu put forward a similar view of the life cycle. He divided human life into four distinct phases.[6] The first encompasses childhood and early adulthood, and is called the "student" or "apprentice" stage. The tasks of this period involve learning about the world, and particularly about social duties. (Mastering social roles, with the associated "masks" discussed in conjunction with "The Magic Towel," falls into this period.) The second phase is that of the "householder," whose responsibilities include earning a living, pursuing a trade, and raising a family. Establishing oneself in society and seeking personal achievements are the goals here—the preoccupations of young adulthood, extending into the middle years.

The third phase of life, according to Manu, begins when the

individual sees his "son's sons." The householder then leaves his family and profession, and retires to live as a hermit in the woods. Through meditation and yoga, the elder ideally transcends an egocentric viewpoint to grasp the mystical unity of the cosmos. Enlightened by this spiritual insight, the individual enters the fourth and final phase of life, wandering the land, emancipated from all desire and suffering.

The traditional views of Confucius and Manu help answer an important question: why self-transcendence is a task for the second half of life, and not the first. The challenge of youth is to establish a strong sense of self and to learn the ways of the world. Only after developing a self is self-transcendence possible,[7] and only after experiencing material satisfactions can the individual truly give them up.

The tale of Parsifal, which is part of the legends surrounding King Arthur, conveys these insights quite well.[8] The story is important because it comes from a Western perspective, and yet independently echoes the teachings of Confucius and Manu. As a youth, Parsifal stumbles upon the Castle of the Holy Grail, and beholds the Grail itself. But Parsifal does not know what to do there (he needs to ask three crucial questions), and so is summarily expelled from the Grail Castle. The experience nevertheless inspires him to become a knight, and he becomes one of the champions of the Round Table. Parsifal's early encounter with the Holy Grail symbolizes the visions which inspire adolescents—ideals about truth, justice, and God—but which they often do not know how to handle. Indeed, *the* task of youth can be said to be translating lofty visions into practical pursuits,[9] transforming inspiration into dedication.

Many years later, at the height of his fame, Parsifal is summoned again to seek the Holy Grail. He abandons the power and prestige of King Arthur's court to struggle through foreign countries on a renewed religious quest. Eventually Parsifal finds the Grail Castle and beholds the Holy Grail again. This second time he knows what to do, and he redeems himself and his country. In maturity, Parsifal can understand and benefit from the spiritual revelation that baffled him in youth.

The same pattern can be seen in the lives of modern adults. A variety of studies have shown that men and women become practical and worldly in the middle years, only to shift later in life, and return to humanitarian, moral, and religious issues.[10] The resurgence in religious interests, moreover, is not merely due to illness and fear of death, as has sometimes been suggested—a desperate turn to religion when other coping mechanisms fail. Quite the contrary holds. For instance, in a recent study of 836 men and women from the ages of 55 to 94, greater interest in spiritual matters correlated with better morale and psychological adjustment, and the correlation was even stronger for older adults.[11] But religious concerns often take new and more personal forms in later life: private reflections at home, for instance, rather than public attendance at church or synagogue.[12]

The return to spiritual concerns in the second half of life is most dramatic in the lives of great scientists and thinkers. Alfred North Whitehead, a mathematician-philosopher, provides an excellent example.[13] Like other teenagers, Whitehead was profoundly moved by religious questions in his adolescence and struggled many years with them. In college, however, he gave up his religious pursuits and became a mathematician. The high point of his mathematical work was writing the *Principia Mathematica* with Bertrand Russell, in which they derived all of arithmetic and algebra from a few basic principles of logic. Their *magnum opus* is still considered a model of rigorous, rational scientific thinking.

After a long and illustrious career, Whitehead retired from his academic post in Britain, only to begin writing essays in metaphysics of almost mystical inclination. Like Parsifal, Whitehead could not grapple directly with spiritual issues in his youth, but years of experience and learning enabled him to do so in maturity. Indeed, Whitehead's theological work from late in his life has had a lasting impact on contemporary thought—more, ironically, than his earlier mathematical writing. And Whitehead is not an isolated example. From Newton to Einstein, great scientists have often embraced in later life the spiritual concerns they put aside in their youth.

Many writers and artists exhibit a kindred course of development. Tolstoy, for example, devoted himself to worldy pursuits as a military officer in the first half of life, and then became a justly famous writer. At fifty, however, he suffered a deep personal crisis despite his many successes and fell into despair over the meaning-lessness of his life. He subsequently devoted himself to religious concerns of mystical depth.[14] A similar development can be observed in musicians, including Beethoven,[15] and such artists as Rembrandt, Michelangelo, Donatello, Titian, and El Greco.[16] Indeed, the late-life styles of many painters are similar, and have been described as "transcendent," or inspired by "ultimate revela-tion." If spiritual transcendence is a task of later life, then the form of such development can vary widely, depending on the individ-ual's background and temperament.

One last point deserves mention in our story. "An Old Moth-er's Sorrow" revolves around the theme of death. Surprisingly, this motif is rare in elder tales. In fact, death figures more promi-nently in tales of youth. In the Italian story, "The Land Where No One Dies," for example, and the Japanese tale, "The Man Who Did Not Wish to Die,"[17] the protagonists are explicitly identified as being around thirty years old. Moreover, protagonists who seek immortality are generally young adults. Paradoxically, in fairy tales death is more disturbing to youth than to older adults.

A French fairy story, Laboulaye's "The Castle of Life,"[18] makes the point quite nicely. In the tale, an old grandmother saves three fairies from a horrible fate. They bestow on her one wish, and tell her she can ask for anything she wants. She thinks of eternal youth, but decides she has seen as much of the world as she wants. So she gives the wish to her grandson (note her generativ-ity), and he promptly wishes she could live forever, because he needs her (note his self-seeking). The youth fears her death more than the old woman does.

Do elder tales simply deny the reality of death? The answer is "no." Elder tales do not depict immortality and eternal youth as an ending. Instead, they portray the death of the protagonist as a simple fact, the way the present tale does—"On the third day she died." In fact, "He lived in comfort until the day he died," or "She died in peace," is a common ending to elder tales. These stories accept death as part of the natural life cycle: their protagonists inhabit the "ever after," not the "forever after." "An Old Mother's Sorrow" helps us understand this calm acceptance. It is a product of self-transcendence. Death is a problem only if the individual clings to an egocentric viewpoint and values his or her own life above all else. Surveys of older adults document the truth of these fairy tale insights: fear of death subsides with maturity and there are suggestions that equanimity toward death correlates with mental health.[19] Death simply becomes another fact of life to the mature individual.

If religious forms of self-transcendence dominated societies in the past, they do not now. Modern culture is inspired more by technology than theology, and the spiritual teachings of the past, though rich and deep, are often difficult to apply in today's secular world. Yet the challenge is neither insurmountable nor even new. Each era must reinterpret its traditions to fit changing realities, and elder tales offer help with the task by portraying *secular* versions of transcendence, as we shall see in the next story.

9

The Dragon King
of the Sea

(a Korean story)

nce upon a time, a poor old fisherman lived with his wife at the edge of the sea. One day, no matter what he did, he could not catch anything. He was about to leave in despair, when he decided to try one last time. To his astonishment, he caught a large fish, more beautiful than any he had ever seen. The fish looked at him with eyes that were so human, the old fisherman did not have the heart to kill the creature. So he let it go.

The next day, as the old man was fishing, a little boy stepped out of the ocean. He invited the astonished fisherman to the palace of the Dragon King in the sea. The boy explained that the Dragon King wanted to thank the fisherman for sparing the life of his son the day before. Then the waves parted, revealing a road into the ocean, and the old man followed the little boy.

The fisherman soon arrived at a magnificent palace, where the Dragon King and his son greeted the old man warmly. Servants appeared and set out a royal feast for the old man, complete with dancers, singers, and jugglers. The fisherman enjoyed himself so much he hardly noticed the time passing, but he suddenly remembered his wife. So he arose and asked leave to return home. At this point, the

Prince sidled up to the fisherman. "My father will offer you anything you wish as a gift. Be sure to ask for the measuring cup that he keeps beside his throne. It is magic and will give you whatever you wish for."

Sure enough, as a token of his gratitude, the Dragon King offered the fisherman anything he desired. The old man asked for the magic cup, and the Dragon King hesitated. So the Prince asked, "Which is more valuable, dear father? My life or the measuring cup?" So the Dragon King gave the cup to the fisherman.

When the old man returned home, he told his wife about his adventure. They marvelled at the magic cup, and then they decided to try it out. So they wished for a new house, and in an instant, a beautiful home appeared in place of their old hut. From then on, the old man and his wife lived in comfort, and their magic cup was always full of rice, no matter how much they took from it.

One day, a wicked woman came calling. She had heard rumors about the magic cup that was always full of rice, and she wanted to find out where the old couple kept it hidden, so she could steal it. The villain showed the fisherman's wife some jewels and offered to trade them for rice. So the old woman fetched the magic cup, and filled a bag with rice. The wicked lady carefully noted where the old woman put the magic measure. Later that night, a thief broke into the house and stole the cup. Without its magic, the old man and woman soon became as poor as ever.

Now the old couple had a dog and a cat, and the two animals felt badly for their master and mistress. So they decided to search for the cup. They suspected that the wicked woman had stolen it, so one evening they followed her as she went about her business. When darkness fell, she left the village and swam across a river, making her way to a house hidden in the forest. This was the home of an infamous thief, and the cat and dog deduced he had stolen the magic cup. The woman and the thief soon left, so the cat and dog prowled around the house and found a locked storeroom.

"The cup must be in there!" the dog exclaimed, and they tried to break in, but to no avail. Then they saw a rat scurry by, and the cat caught it. The cat threatened to kill the rat unless the King of the Rats appeared, and the King soon did. So the cat made him promise to break into the storeroom, and the Rat King called all his subjects. They quickly nibbled a hole in the wall, large enough for the cat and dog to enter. In the storeroom the two animals found a stone chest, locked securely. So they asked the rats to open it, and the rats fell upon the box, and soon gnawed a hole in it. And there inside lay the magic cup! The dog and cat grabbed it and hurried out of the house.

When they came to the river, the dog swam across with the cat on his back, and the cup in the cat's mouth. Midway across the water the dog became anxious and asked, "Do you still have the cup?" The cat could not reply since he held the cup in his mouth, so the dog asked again and again. Finally the cat said, "Yes, I do!" But when the cat opened its mouth, the cup fell out and sank in the river.

The two animals were mortified, and the dog went home in despair. Meanwhile, the cat searched the river banks, hoping that the magic cup might wash ashore. He only found a dead fish, but he took it and gave it to the old woman. At least, he reasoned, she would have something to cook. But when the old woman cut the fish to clean it, the magic cup rolled out of its stomach! The fish had swallowed the cup when the measure fell into the river.

The old man and woman soon lived in comfort again, and they honored their cat and dog. But this time, they also kept the magic measure hidden in a very safe place!

Summarized from "The Cat and the Dog," in Z. In-Sob, ed., Folk Tales from Korea *(New York: Grove, 1979); a similar story can be found in F. H. Mayer,* Ancient Tales in Modern Japan *(Bloomington, Ind.: Indiana University Press, 1985).*

Reflections: Transcendence and the Inner Self

This story is filled with many odd details that make its meaning seem elusive at first. But the details elaborate steadily upon an important new motif—a secular form of transcendence.

The tale starts with an old man who is quite poor, presenting the usual theme of loss. The story also specifies that the old man is a fisherman. This occupation appears frequently in elder tales, suggesting that fishing symbolizes something about the psychology of aging. (We first saw the theme in "The Magic Forest," where the old woman goes to fetch a fish from the lake.) Consider first the symbolism of the ocean: dark, unknown, and teeming with hidden forms of life, it often appears in dreams as a symbol of the unconscious, in exactly the same way that a forest does.[1] Since fishermen catch things from the sea, they symbolize the process of retrieving material from the unconscious. And this is the central focus of the story.

After a day of particularly bad luck, the fisherman catches a fish, but with eyes so human and sad, the fisherman lets it go out of pity. This event triggers the whole drama of the story, and is heavily symbolic. First of all, in releasing the fish, the old man breaks his usual practice. He has caught and killed fish for many years, so his sudden change of behavior is surprising. A similar event occurs in "Fortune and the Woodcutter," where the old woodcutter suddenly and uncharacteristically stops working. The theme appears in other elder tales, suggesting that the motif is significant.

One interpretation of the theme comes from the psychologist Robert Peck.[2] He studied men and women in the second half of life, and tried to distinguish those who did well as they aged from those who did not. He noted that most adults identify themselves by their roles—what they do or to whom they are related. "I am a teacher," a person may say, or "I am Jo's husband." Peck found that individuals who were flexible enough to break free of such a conventional social identity did better in later life. Other researchers have independently made similar observations.[3] Mature individuals distinguish between social roles and the inner self, and so are more able to adopt different roles and adapt to changing circumstances. The story symbolizes the process through the old man letting the fish go. He breaks out of his customary identity as a fisherman and thus becomes open to new developments. (In just the same way, the old man in "Fortune and the Woodcutter" abandons his role as a woodcutter and so paves the way for Fortune to come to him.)

The story notes that the old man releases the fish because he feels pity and compassion for the poor creature. This is surprising since the old man has had to kill fish throughout his life to make a living. He may have felt mercy for fish before, but he could not afford to heed the sentiment. Now he does, and he attends to a new side of his nature—a tender, compassionate one, which was hidden before. The same theme surfaces in other elder tales, like the Japanese story, "The Demon with Eight Faces," or the Estonian tale, "The Kind Woodcutter."[4] So this motif, too, is likely to have special significance.

Jung's researches offer an interpretation. He observed that in youth, individuals are forced to repress or neglect certain aspects of their personalities. Boys, for instance, are usually discouraged from being too soft-hearted, and quickly learn to suppress their compassionate side, which then becomes unconscious. Conversely, girls are criticized if they are too assertive, or independent, and rapidly learn to conform to social norms. In the second half of life, these neglected sides of the personality clamor for a place in conscious life. The challenge of maturity, Jung argued, is to reclaim these forgotten aspects. If the individual succeeds, the outcome is psychological balance and inner wholeness.[5]

Typically, Jung observed, from mid-life onward men attend to their tender, nurturant feelings, spending less time at the office making money, for example, and more at home with the family. Conversely, women reclaim their assertiveness and autonomy, perhaps embarking on business careers after raising their children.[6] Others have confirmed Jung's observations in more systematic studies. Indeed, the pattern can be seen in different American socioeconomic classes,[7] and in cultures from Native American tribes to Polynesian societies and African communities.[8] These role reversals also go beyond gender stereotypes. Men who have been passive and unassertive in youth often become aggressive in later life, and women who have been aggressive—successful women executives, for instance—reclaim their nurturing, affiliative sides.[9] The central process here is that of balance, of integrating forgotten aspects of the personality and achieving greater wholeness.

In this story, a young boy steps out of the ocean and greets the old man. Assuming that the boy symbolizes a psychological event, one possible interpretation is that he represents the "inner child" in adults—what Jung called the Puer, or archetypal youth.[10] This inner child takes many forms in adult life, sometimes in unpleasant ways—in tantrums or whining—and sometimes in positive forms—in innocence, playfulness, and creativity. (This is the difference between being child*ish* and child*like*.) Because adults are expected to conform to social norms, the inner child remains unconscious for the most part in daily life. By portraying a little boy stepping out of the sea, our story hints that the reclamation of the inner child is an important task for maturity. Indeed, Levinson found just this in his study of the mid-life transition,[11] a time when individuals struggle with the polarity between youth and old age, trying to balance the innocence and spontaneity of the former with the soberness and sagacity of the latter.

Reclaiming the spirit of youth is a theme that appears repeatedly in elder tales. In the story "The Magic Forest," for example, elves leap out of the magic kindling and act like innocent, playful children. They symbolize the return of a youthful spirit and even have childlike names, too—"Wee Tintilinki," for example. Moreover, the elves take the old woman back to happy memories of her childhood. As we shall see, similar events occur in other elder tales.

In the present story, the little boy takes the old man to visit the Dragon King, deep in the sea. This is the crux of the story, and the king is clearly an important symbolic figure. First of all, in the mythology of East Asia the dragon is one of the most beneficent creatures, the ruler of the zodiac and the symbol of the creative spirit. (This view contrasts sharply with Western tradition portraying dragons as evil monsters, but Eastern mythology retains the awesome, frightening aspect of the dragon.) The Dragon King apparently lives in infinite wealth and can provide anything a person wants with his magic cup. Because concrete facts often symbolize psychological states in fairy tales, it is reasonable to interpret the Dragon King's material wealth as a symbol for psychological wealth. He can then be taken as a symbol of psychological completion and wholeness, the reclamation and integration of all aspects of human nature. This is obviously an ideal, since no one person can attain such complete wholeness. So the Dragon King symbolizes *mankind*'s highest potential, hidden within the unconscious. (In Chinese tradition, the dragon is the symbol of the emperor, who in turn represents the highest ideals of humanity.)

Psychoanalysts like Jung and Assagioli[12] called this image of psychological wholeness "the inner Self" or "the higher Self," using a capital S to distinguish it from our usual conscious sense of "self." The latter is the self we refer to when we say, "I am a teacher" or "I am tired"—the "I" of conscious thinking, which psychologists usually call the "ego." In traditional religious terms, the higher Self would correspond most closely with the soul or spirit, the deepest center of wholeness in any individual.

Jung argued that the search for the Self is *the* task for the second half of life.[13] This endeavor may seem narcissistic—a preoccupation with self-fulfillment—but quite the contrary holds. When an individual encounters the higher Self, the experience is humbling because the person glimpses the noblest potential of mankind. He is thus forced to recognize the limits of his own conscious ego—how small he is, compared to what humankind can be. Indeed, confronting the inner Self is a transcendent experience in two senses. First, it requires the individual to transcend conscious identity, the self with the small s, the "I" defined by social custom and personal beliefs. And second, the encounter usually has a numinous quality to it: it is a deeply moving and inspirational experience.

"The Measuring Cup" does not end with this transcendent development, however. It is an unusually well-balanced tale and goes on to describe how a greedy younger woman steals the magic cup from the old man and his wife. This raises the theme of generational conflict we saw in "The Wise Merchant." Unlike the old merchant, though, the old couple lack the wisdom to protect themselves. So their dog and cat come to the rescue, aided by rats. These ordinary animals contrast dramatically with the sublime figure of the Dragon King, but the point is symbolic. Contact with the inner Self is inspiring and deeply moving, but unless the experience is grounded in practical human realities, trouble results. Without the earthy abilities of the cat, the dog, and especially the rats, the old man and woman would have permanently lost the treasure of the Dragon King. The story thus underscores the importance of worldly wisdom in later life, for it provides pragmatic grounding for transcendent experiences. The cup itself is a good symbol of practical wisdom. It is a *measuring* cup, and as such, connotes the capacity to set limits, to balance, and to make discriminations.

Perhaps the most dramatic confirmation of the insights in this tale comes from a real-life example. Mr. R consulted me about depression when he was in his early 50's, and the course of his therapy involved a journey to the inner Self that closely paralleled the tale of "The Dragon King." Initially, Mr. R struggled with deciding whether he wanted to continue in his highly successful business or change his career, plagued as he was by a vague sense of mid-life dissatisfaction. He decided to abandon his commercial endeavor and started working with troubled youth. During this period of radical change, he had a striking dream in which he walked along a road on his way to meet a woman he had known for many years. When he arrived at her house, he found a marvelous palace in place of her real home. The palace was made of glass and crystal, and glittered magically in the daylight. Mr. R's friend greeted him at the door and ushered him in, leading him on a tour of the palace. Room after room was filled with beautiful flowers and priceless antiques. Then the woman gave Mr. R a huge gold key and told him it was the key to the palace. At this point Mr. R woke up, deeply inspired by the dream.

Mr. R's dream during his mid-life change mirrors the tale of "The Dragon King of the Sea." As he shifted his career from business to counseling troubled youth, Mr. R began reclaiming the nurturing, caring feelings which he had suppressed in his commercial endeavors, just as the old fisherman embraced compassionate sentiments in the story. Mr. R's dream symbolized the development through his visit to a woman friend, who personified his feminine side. Similarly, the story depicts the fisherman sparing the life of the fish. In Mr. R's dream, he next arrives at a home so magnificent that it is really a palace, filled with treasure. The house recalls the residence of the Dragon King and, indeed, both places symbolize the inner Self—an ideal of integration and harmony deep within the unconscious, rich with human potential. Mr. R's friend then gives him the golden key, just as the Dragon King gives the fisherman the measuring cup. The objects symbolize a new, vital connection to the transcendent realm of the inner Self.

While Mr. R's dream ended here, his real-life drama did not. With great enthusiasm and inspiration, he took several troubled teenagers into his own home, trying to help them start anew in life. Several of them stole things and then vanished. He was robbed, just like the old man and his wife in the tale. Mr. R quickly realized he had become careless in the ways of the world, forgetting what he had learned from many years in business, so taken was he by his inner inspirations. Sobered by his initial experience with wayward youth, Mr. R became more careful—and more successful. He integrated his altruistic new inspirations with practical wisdom, just the way the old couple learned to protect the magic gift of the Dragon King with the earthy cunning of the cat, the dog, and the rats.

The story of the old fisherman and the tale of Mr. R depict a special form of self-transcendence. The old man abandons his customary identity as a fisherman, transcending social convention and personal beliefs. He then encounters an inner source of transcendent wholeness—the higher Self. This process of self-transcendence contrasts with that portrayed in "The Magic Forest," and "An Old Mother's Sorrow." We might therefore compare these three forms of transcendent experience.

In "The Magic Forest," the widow puts aside her own sorrows for the sake of her son and her altruism ultimately emancipates society from magic. So the old woman's self-transcendence is *interpersonal and social.* In "An Old Mother's Sorrow," the old woman breaks out of her personal grief, inspired by a religious vision in which she sees her part in God's plan. Self-transcendence here is *introspective and religious.* In the present tale, the old man abandons his conscious psychological identity to glimpse the full potential of human nature. His experience of self-transcendence is *introspective and psychological.* Depending upon the individual's inclination and background, self-transcendence involves God, Society, or Self.[14]

Transcendence in its many forms initiates a special kind of growth that can be called "transpersonal development."[15] The term quite literally refers to development that transcends, or goes beyond (the meaning of the Latin root, *trans*), our familiar conscious personalities (or *person*). While the phrase may seem awkward or even pretentious at first, it serves a useful function. It highlights what sacred and secular traditions hold in common: the quest for something beyond the finite self, whether that is God, Society, or Self. "Transpersonal development" offers a neutral idiom for our modern era, allowing us to avoid the embarrassment that religious language sometimes engenders in secular society, while reminding us of deeply human experiences which a purely secular approach often ignores.

Recognizing this transpersonal dimension of development opens up new realms of experience and offers rich resources for guidance in the second half of life—literature, philosophy, art, and mythology. These are the disciplines which look most deeply into human experience and grapple with transcendent insights. They first become important in youth, when heroic ideals and lofty visions help young men and women define their goals and values in life. In maturity, these ideals regain their significance, but in a new way—they help the adult transcend the self, not find it. And the mature individual does not seek a place in society, as young men and women do, but rather the place of society within human history, and of human history in the cosmos.

10

The Old Man Who Lost His Wen

(from Japan)

Long ago and far away, there lived an old man and his wife near a forest. The old man was a handsome fellow in his youth, but as he grew older, an ugly wen appeared on his face, becoming larger and larger with age. Over the years, he went to doctors and magicians, and tried potions and powders, but nothing helped. At last he resigned himself to the wen, and he even tried to joke about it.

One day, the old man needed some firewood, so he hiked into the mountains and chopped some wood. It was a crisp autumn day, and he enjoyed himself so much that he did not notice the storm clouds gathering. When the first raindrops hit him, the old man looked hastily for shelter. He found a hollow tree and climbed inside, just as the storm arrived. Thunder shook the mountains, and lightning flashed around him, but he remained safe and dry. After several hours, the storm passed and the old man emerged from his haven. In the distance he heard voices and so he thought his neighbors had come searching for him. But when he looked, he gasped with horror—a horde of demons and goblins approached!

The old man hastily retreated into the tree, trembling with fear. The demons arrived, and one goblin, more horrifying than the others and evidently their leader, motioned to his followers. "Let us have our feast here," he said. Then the demon king sat down right in front of the hollow tree, with his back to the old man. The poor man nearly fainted with terror.

The demons quickly spread out a picnic, and then began singing. The old man stared in astonishment, never having seen anything like it before. But when the demons started dancing, he could not help laughing. They were clumsy and awkward, and they all looked ridiculous, prancing about and falling down. Finally the king of the demons motioned for his dancers to stop. "You are awful!" the king complained. "Is there no one here who knows how to dance properly?"

Now the old man loved dancing, and he was quite good at it. "I could teach them a thing or two," he thought to himself, but he dared not show himself, fearing that the demons would kill him. The demon king asked again if anybody knew how to dance, and the old man was torn between his love of dancing, and his fear of the demons. The goblin king asked a third time, and the old man threw caution to the wind.

He stepped out of the tree, and bowed to the chief of the demons. "I can dance, my lord," the old man said, and proceeded to do so. The demons were scandalized at having a man in their midst, but they soon admired the old man's dancing. They started tapping their hooves in time to the music, and some demons even joined the old man. For his part, the old man realized that his life depended on dancing well, so he put his whole heart and spirit into his movements, and enjoyed himself thoroughly. When he paused, the demon king applauded, and invited the old man to sit next to him, offering a cup of wine.

"You must come back tomorrow to dance for us," the demon king said.

"I would love to," the old man replied.

One of the king's advisor's spoke up. "You can't trust humans. We must take something to guarantee he will return." Unfortunately, the old man had nothing valuable with him.

"Well, then," the demon king said, "I will take this as a pledge," and he reached out and grasped the old man's wen, plucking it off as easily as a ripe peach. "Mind you return tomorrow," the demon king said, and all the goblins vanished.

The old man could scarcely believe what happened. He reached up and felt how smooth his cheeks were—and symmetrical! He was so happy, he ran home, skipping, singing—and dancing—all the way. His wife was overjoyed to see him without his wen, and they celebrated his good fortune.

Now the old man had a wicked, vain neighbor who also had a wen, and who never gave up seeking a cure for it. When the neighbor heard all the festivities, he came prying and was astonished to see the old man's wen was gone. The vain man immediately asked what happened, so the old man told his story about the demons. The neighbor then insisted that he would go to the goblins the next day, in place of the old man.

So the next morning the vain neighbor went into the mountains, and found the hollowed-out tree, just as the old man had described. And sure enough, at sunset, the demon hordes appeared.

"Where is the old man who will dance for us?" the demon king asked. The wicked neighbor crept out of the tree, trembling with terror. "Here I am!" he said, and proceeded to dance. However, he had never learned how to dance, thinking it beneath his dignity, and so he merely hopped around and flapped his arms. He thought the demons would not know the difference, but the king was offended.

"This is terrible!" the goblin king exclaimed, "you are not dancing at all like yesterday!" The king did not realize he dealt with a different man because humans all looked alike to him. "I can't stand it!" the demon king cried out at last. He reached in his pocket and drew out the wen. "Here, I give you back your guarantee." With that, the demon king threw the wen at the vain man and it stuck to his face. Then the demons vanished. In horror, the vain man felt his cheeks and sure enough, he had two wens, one on each side! He sneaked home late that night, and no one ever saw his face again, because from then on he wore a large hat pulled low on his head.

As for the old man who lost his wen, he lived to a good age and he danced whenever he felt happy. And that was often indeed!

Summarized from "How an Old Man Lost His Wen" adapted from Y. T. Ozaki, The Japanese Fairy Book *(Tokyo: Tuttle, 1970); and Y. Yasuda,* Old Tales of Japan *(Tokyo: Tuttle, 1965).*

Reflections: Emancipated Innocence

The wen is the most dramatic symbol in this tale, tying several themes together like a knot. It is thus the key to the tale. The old man, we are told, was not born with the disfigurement. The wretched thing appeared when he was an adult and grew bigger as he grew older. A natural interpretation, then, is that the wen represents the blemishes of aging—wrinkles, liver spots, and so on. But there is a deeper meaning here, and the clue to it can be found in a comment by the playwright George Bernard Shaw: "Anyone over forty has the face they deserve." While age alone makes its mark on the face, habitual moods do so even more sharply. Constant worries wrinkle the brow, and unrelenting anger sours the mouth. In maturity the face becomes a book in which one's humor, good or bad, is inscribed.[1] This suggests that the wen—something ugly on the outside—symbolizes something wretched on the inside. We saw just this theme in the tale of "The Magic Towel," where the nasty old woman's face became hideous, revealing the wickedness of her heart. Indeed, in most tales of youth, external ugliness represents inner evil.[2]

The present story is an elder tale, however, and it makes clear that the old man is not truly evil. To underscore the point, the tale throws in a real villain—the vain neighbor. So what might the wen signify?

Because the wen plagued the old man only in his adult years, it must refer to some ugliness associated with adult life, rather than youth or childhood. This brings up an age-old theme—the belief that children are innocent, not yet having learned to lie, cheat, or disguise their feelings. By maturity most individuals have fallen from grace, like the biblical Adam and Eve, and the wen symbolizes the inevitable ugliness of adult life: white lies, angry outbursts, or compromises in honor. The story also says— and this is important—that the old man resigned himself to his disfigurement after many years of trying to get rid of it. He accepted his blemish with good grace. This brings up another familiar theme in elder tales—that of self-confrontation and self-reformation. The old man has come to terms with his outward blemish and thus, we can infer, with his vanity and inner ugliness, too. To highlight the point, the story contrasts him with his neighbor, who is not able to transcend his vanity or accept his deformity, and who is accordingly called "wicked."

The story takes place high in the mountains, repeating two common elements of elder tales, a woodcutter, and a journey into the forest, both of which symbolize the process of reaching into the unconscious. The appearance of demons confirms this symbolism, since demons are creatures of the underworld, and the underworld is usually equated with the unconscious in interpretations of mythology.[3] The old man is initially terrified of the demons, and hides from them. So what happens next is astonishing and crucial: he steps out of his hiding place to dance with the demons. What might his action symbolize?

The clue lies in what happens after he finishes his dance: the demon king removes the wen from the old man. The old man thus regains his original unblemished appearance—the face he had as a child. The event symbolizes, I suggest, the old man's reclamation of childhood innocence. Indeed, he dances wholeheartedly, for the sheer joy of dancing, the way a child plays—with zest, spontaneity, glee, and innocence.

This interpretation would be tenuous if it were based only on this story. But we have already met the theme of reclaiming childlike innocence in "The Dragon King of the Sea." There a little boy emerges from the ocean, symbolizing the appearance of the inner child from the unconscious. The elves play a similar role in "The Magic Forest," and as we shall see, other elder tales repeat the motif in still more creative forms. Taken together, elder tales suggest that the restoration of innocence is a major task in later life.

The present story highlights two points about this process of reclamation. First, in dancing with the demons, the old man throws caution and rationality to the wind. He ignores the conventional view that demons are dangerous, as well as the usual adult concerns with looking foolish. In other words, he *emancipates* himself from social convention and rational thinking. Indeed, the demons can be interpreted as a symbol of everything that violates the rules of civilized society. They are Dionysiac figures and represent the spontaneous, uninhibited power of nature. (The thunderstorm preceding the demons' appearance has similar connotations. This story, like a dream, repeats its message in different symbolic details.)

If the old man abandons social conventions, he does not sacrifice reason. Like the wise merchant in the story of that name, this old man is not naive. He recognizes his peril: if he offends the demons, or bores them, he knows they might tear him to pieces. So he concentrates on his performance and uses skills that only long practice provides. This is the second feature of the old man's spontaneity: in emancipating himself from social convention, the old man does not *eliminate* adult rationality. He *adds* spontaneity and innocence to mature judgment and skill.

Innocence with judgment, spontaneity with skill, that is the paradox of the old man's attitude. We can call this spirit "emancipated innocence," and its development is a task for later life, one that many cultures implicitly recognize. In Japan, for example, from whence the present story comes, childhood and old age are the two times when an individual is exempted from rigid social conventions. When a person turns 60, friends and family celebrate with a ceremony in which the 60-year-old dons a special red garment. The robe signifies the elder's emancipation from social obligations, and a return to the freedom of childhood.[4] At the same time, the elder is expected to be wise and spiritually advanced. In a similar vein, the Balinese say that young children and old people are the closest to divinity because children have only recently left the innocence and magic of Heaven, while elders will soon return to it.[5]

On the other side of the world, a similar development occurs among the !Kung tribesmen in Africa. Many adults start to dance and play enthusiastically in later life, freed from social obligations and conventions.[6] In one tribe, an anthropologist noted a woman over 60 gleefully jumping rope with a group of girls. And an old !Kung man was famous in his tribe for hilarious and spontaneous dancing.

Emancipated innocence can be seen in Western culture, although there may be less explicit social encouragement of the attitude. As one 72-year-old woman put it, "At my age, I can do anything and say anything I want! I don't worry about what other people think, the way I used to. And the best part is that people accept me anyway!" Her sentiments echo the feelings of many older individuals revealed in more systematic research studies. Old age gives the individual a socially accepted "excuse" to ignore normal conventions. And this freedom is an important benefit of aging in many cultures.[7]

A caveat is important here. Social conventions have a purpose: they force everyone to respect each other and thus help reduce conflicts. If an individual abandons these conventions, and simply does what he wishes, he easily becomes selfish, opinionated, and rude. Emancipated innocence implies that the individual first comes to terms with his own egocentricity. Self-confrontation and self-transcendence make the difference between *childlike* innocence and *childishness.* The story underscores the point with a tiny detail already mentioned: the old man has accepted his deformity. He has transcended his vanity. Emancipated innocence is not simply license to do as one pleases—it is the challenge of transcending personal desires and social conventions.

A dramatic illustration of emancipated innocence can be found in the life of Carl Jung. At mid-life, after many fruitful years

81

of working together, Jung broke with Freud, his mentor, in an acrimonious dispute. Uncertain of his own direction, Jung drifted for some time. During this period he felt a strange, baffling urge to play with stones on a lakeshore[8] and spent hours building little castles and houses, just as he had when he was a child. At this time, Jung began elaborating his own theories of human nature, and embarked upon an extraordinarily creative period of work, emancipating himself from prevailing social and religious traditions. Childlike innocence, spontaneous play, and liberation from established conventions converged in his experience of emancipated innocence.

Jung is not alone in illustrating this development. Paul Gauguin, the famous 19th century French painter, provides another example. A stockbroker by profession, Gauguin suffered a business reversal at mid-life in a market crash. He then decided, against all pragmatic considerations, to pursue his painting without any means of earning a living, and with a family to support. He lost both family and reputation as a result. His wife divorced him, and his former acquaintances repudiated him. But he persisted, and created his own distinctive style of painting. He rejected the refined artistry of his period—Impressionism—and turned instead to "primitive" art. He lived many years in the South Pacific among the Polynesians, fascinated by what he perceived as their innocence. Gauguin soon captured this spirit in his paintings, but his art was hardly childlike. He executed his works with great thought and care, and infused them with deep symbolic meanings—the innocent style of his art was the product of mature skill. Like the old man who danced with the demons, Gauguin reclaimed his childlike innocence through the sophisticated means of art.

A more systematic investigation of emancipated innocence comes from the psychologist Abraham Maslow, who studied unusually mature individuals. Although not specifically researching the psychology of aging, Maslow found that the individuals meeting his criteria for extraordinary psychological health were all over 50. This in itself is noteworthy. But what is more important are the characteristics these individuals shared. They were what Maslow called "self-actualizing"—realizing their full personal potential. These men and women typically broke from cultural norms to pursue their own creative insights, emancipating themselves from convention and ordinary "rationality." But they also transcended their own egocentric concerns. They could absorb themselves in their work, for instance, and pursue projects, irrespective of public reward for their efforts. Personal recognition mattered less than the creative work itself. And these self-actualizing individuals acted in a spontaneous, expressive way that recalled the innocence and liveliness of children. Maslow emphasized the paradox of this innocence, because it integrated naivete with mature judgment. "If children are 'naive,' " Maslow wrote, "then my subjects had attained a 'second naivete' as Santayana called it. Their innocence of perception and experience was combined with sophisticated minds."[9] Others have since corroborated Maslow's findings,[10] underscoring the importance of emancipated innocence as a task of maturity.

Although magical, the story of the old man with the wen is more than a fairy tale. It reflects a lofty potential of human development that can be seen in different cultures around the world—a vision of what mature adults can aspire to, and an alternative to the specter of decline.

11
The Simple Grasscutter
(from India)

ar away and long ago, an old man lived alone at the edge of a jungle, earning his living by cutting grass for fodder. He lived a simple life and saved most of his meager income in a pot. One night, he wondered how much money he had accumulated through the years, and when he looked in his pot, he was astonished to discover a goodly sum. He rubbed his head, wondering what to do with his small fortune. He did not desire more than what he already possessed, nor did he want the pennies to sit unused. Then he had an idea.

The next day the old man went to a jeweler, and bought a beautiful gold bracelet. He visited a friend who was a merchant and asked, "Who is the most beautiful and virtuous woman in the world?"

The merchant immediately answered, "It is the Princess of the East!"

"Then take this bracelet to her," the old grasscutter said, "and tell her only that it is a gift from one who admires beauty and virtue."

The merchant left on one of his many voyages and soon enough came to the palace of the Princess. He gave her the bracelet and the old man's message. The Princess was delighted by the lovely gift, but puzzled by the anonymity of the giver. She sent a present in return anyway—bolts of precious cloth. The merchant returned to the grasscutter and presented him with the rolls of silk.

The old man did not know what to do with the precious cloth and had no desire to keep them. So he asked his friend, "Who is the most handsome and virtuous man in the world? Surely he can use these more than me!"

"That would be the Prince of the West," the merchant replied, and at the old man's request, he took the precious cloth to the noble young man. The Prince was perplexed by the anonymous gift, but he gave the merchant a dozen thoroughbred horses in return.

"What am I to do with them!" the old man exclaimed when his friend presented him with the horses. Then the grasscutter had an idea. "Keep two horses for yourself, my friend, and take the rest to the Princess of the East. She will care for them better than I can."

The merchant laughed, and travelled to the east, giving the horses to the Princess. Perplexed by the new and even more generous gift, she asked her father what to do. "Return a present so magnificent," he said, "your admirer will be ashamed to send anything more! And that will be the end of the matter." So the Princess entrusted the merchant with twenty mules, each loaded with silver.

"Twenty mules all with silver!" the old man exclaimed when his friend returned. "What am I to do with them?" So the old man asked his friend to keep six of the animals with all their treasure, and take the rest to the Prince of the West.

When the Prince saw the sumptuous gift, he was astonished. Not to be outdone, he sent back twenty camels and twenty elephants, each loaded with precious gifts. When his friend returned with the caravan the grasscutter exclaimed, "There is only one thing to do!" And the old man asked the merchant to keep two camels and two elephants, and then lead the rest to the Princess of the East.

When the merchant arrived at the palace of the Princess, her father and mother were astounded at the magnificent boon. "This can only mean one thing," the King and Queen told the Princess, "the man wishes to marry you!" So they asked the merchant to conduct them to their daughter's mysterious suitor. The merchant was horrified. If the King and Queen discovered a poor old man was the cause of the whole affair, they would be furious! But the merchant could not refuse the King's request, and he glumly led the royal party on a journey back home.

A day away from the old man's village, the merchant rode ahead to warn his friend. "What are we to do?" the merchant wailed. Then together he and the grasscutter bemoaned their fate, fearing the wrath of the King. Later that night, the merchant returned gloomily to the royal party, and the old grasscutter went to a cliff. It was dark by then, and he wanted to throw himself over the edge. "Better to die by night, than be humiliated in the morning!" he thought. But try as he might, he was too terrified to jump. In utter shame, he collapsed on the ground.

A light then shone from below the cliff, and two angelic beings appeared. "Why do you despair?" they asked the old man, and he explained his situation. The luminous beings smiled, and one of them touched the old man, while the other waved at his hut. In an instant, the old man's rags were changed into rich robes and in place of his shanty there sprang up a magnificent palace. Then the beings vanished.

The old man was dumbfounded and wandered about the palace in confusion. Servants immediately rushed to him and brought him inside, putting him to bed in soft cushions. The next morning, they woke him and dressed him, just as trumpeters sounded a greeting from the palace ramparts. The King and Queen of the East had arrived with their daughter! And leading them was a very perplexed merchant, staring in bewilderment at the new palace. The grasscutter greeted the royal party, while his servants set out a magnificent feast. Then the King approached the old man.

"Do I understand that you wish to marry my daughter?" the King asked. "If so, I heartily agree!"

The old man was astonished, but he declined. "I am too old for her," he said. Then he had an idea. "But I know who will be the perfect husband!" he exclaimed, and so he asked the merchant to invite the Prince of the West for a visit. The Prince arrived and fell in love with the Princess. So the two married in the old man's palace, and everyone celebrated for days on end. Finally the King and Queen departed, and the Prince and Princess, too. But as they rode off, they paused to salute the old man. The King's soldiers sounded a hundred trumpets, and waved a thousand flags. The old man smiled, standing outside his new home. And he bid them all a fond farewell, waving a frond of the freshest and sweetest grass he had gathered that very morning.

Summarized from "Walidad the Simple Hearted," in A. Lang, The Brown Fairy Book *(New York: Longmans, Green, 1914).*

Reflections: Ego-Integrity and Innocence

In its long, enchanting course, this story recapitulates many of the themes that have appeared in previous stories. This repetition is important in two ways. First, it underscores the cross-cultural nature of the motifs in elder tales. And second, it highlights the fact that the themes fall in a certain progression, evident in many different tales. This common sequence suggests that the themes depict a succession of developmental tasks for adulthood: self-reformation comes before self-transcendence, and self-transcendence before emancipated innocence. But emancipated innocence, in turn, leads to a new task which the present story introduces.

The tale begins with a poor old man who has neither wife nor children. So the theme of loss and the fearful image of poverty in old age appear immediately. The old man also lives beside the jungle and cuts grass there for a living. Like woodcutting and fishing, gathering grass in the wilderness symbolizes a process of dealing with the unconscious, and this is the first task of later life.

The old man digs up his life savings, buys a gold bracelet, and asks a friend to give it to the most beautiful and virtuous Princess in the world. Two themes leap out here. First of all, the old man tells his friend to give the gift anonymously. The grasscutter does not seek a gift in return, or some recognition for himself. He simply wants to reward the Princess for her kindness, wisdom, and beauty. The old man's attitude is altruistic and reflects his ability to transcend egocentric desires. His self-transcendence is all the more marked if we compare the old man with gift-giving in tales of youth. Typically, a young hero puts some kind of identifying mark on his gift to a Princess, so she will later recognize him as her benefactor. If she does not, he can at least reclaim the gift! The young man's gift is both a bribe and a calling card. The old man's gift is neither—it is generative. And the development of such altruism is a second task of maturity symbolized in elder tales.

Actually, the old man's action seems foolish. He gives his life savings to a Princess, who hardly needs the gift. Prudence would dictate that he save his money for himself, especially for times when he cannot work. But the old man is no fool. After all, he saved the pennies in the first place, and only a practical and disciplined man could do that. So the grasscutter's action recalls that of the old man who lost his wen. Both men throw caution and prudence to the wind. One dances with demons, and the other gives away his life savings. They act spontaneously, innocently, and—it would seem—foolishly. This, of course, is the spirit of emancipated innocence, elaborated this time in a story from India, rather than Japan. It symbolizes a third task for later life—transcending practical rationality and social convention.

In response to the old man's gift, the Princess reciprocates—and magnificently, too. Fortune unexpectedly falls into the old man's hands, the way it did to the woodcutter in "Fortune and the Woodcutter." But the present tale goes on to tell us what happens *next*, symbolizing a new developmental task.

The old man gives the gifts he receives from the Princess to a distant Prince, and this starts a hilarious cycle of gift-giving. Notice how the drama depends upon an illusion—the old man has the Prince and Princess thinking he is a fabulously wealthy monarch, although he intends no deceit and is not aware of it when it happens. The Prince and Princess cannot imagine their benefactor lives in a hut by the jungle and cuts grass for a living! So we have the theme of illusion, so closely tied up with worldly wisdom. But the key to all the gift-giving lies in the old man's attitude toward the gifts he receives in return. He refuses them, and for very specific reasons which give us the new insights of this tale.

First of all, the old man declines the gifts out of altruism. If we needed further proof that he has transcended selfishness and ego-centricity, here it is. He gives away fabulous wealth, without desiring it for himself. To accentuate the point, we can compare the old man's generativity with the attitude of the young Prince and Princess. When they receive their gifts, they offer presents in return, but for selfish reasons—to maintain their honor and reputations. The Prince and Princess act from pride, power, and etiquette, not altruism. Indeed, if the two had dealt directly with each other, the gift-giving would no doubt have ended quickly, and they would never have met. It is the old man's generativity which brings them together.

Yet there is a deeper meaning to the old man's rejection of the wealth. He chooses to live as he has always lived—simply. He wishes to remain who he is—a simple grasscutter. With the gifts he receives, the old man could build himself a palace, hire hordes of servants, and live like a Rajah. But he chooses not to. The old man's attitude here is profoundly significant. He accepts his life just as he lives it. But his attitude is not one of resignation, despairing of anything better. Nor does he reject the gifts out of bitterness or guilt, feeling they come too late in life for him to enjoy, or that he does not deserve them. The old man refuses the gifts because he has a deep sense of who he is, a strong personal identity. He affirms his life as *his* life. He has no desire to be somebody else. His is a particularly dramatic form of self-acceptance, but fairy tales exaggerate to make a point. What is the message here?

Erik Erikson offers an explanation. As we saw before, Erikson outlined several psychological tasks that adults must master in the second half of life. Generativity is a major one, and the present tale portrays it well. But after generativity comes another, equally important task—the development of what Erikson called "integrity," an attitude of self-acceptance and self-affirmation which might also be called "self-integrity." The mature individual, Erikson argued, must learn to affirm his or her life just as it happened, for better or worse. He must realize that his life history is, to use Erikson's own words, "something that had to be and that by necessity permitted no substitutions."[1] With such integrity, the individual does not compare himself wistfully with other people who may seem more fortunate, or wonder about opportunities missed along the way. He or she does not ask those unanswerable questions, "What if I did this . . . ? What if I did that . . . ?" Instead, the individual says quietly, but firmly, "I am who I am. I have lived as I have lived."

A variety of systematic research has since confirmed Erikson's observations. Integrity and self-acceptance develop with greater maturity. More importantly, they appear to correlate with increased life-satisfaction and better mental health.[2]

A dramatic example of integrity appears in the tale of "The Magic Forest," where the old mother is given a chance to return to the happiest time in her life, through the magic of the Forest King. But she refuses the offer, and chooses to remain who she is and to remember her son. The story explicitly notes that she chooses her own life of sorrow over all the joys in the world, and it is this choice which emancipates the enchanted forest. Like the simple grasscutter, the old mother affirms her life, just as it is, turning down the temptation to live in a magic world. The tale thus illustrates, very subtly, how difficult the task of self-integrity can be. In real life, many individuals choose the magic world of memories, inhabiting the past rather than facing the present.

"The Simple Grasscutter" elaborates several important aspects of self-integrity. First of all, there is a close connection between integrity and emancipated innocence. After all, it is the old man's act of emancipated innocence—giving the Princess his life savings—which starts everything off. He receives more and more gifts in return, and they offer the old man an alternative to his impoverished life. Only with such an opportunity can he authentically affirm, or reject, his life. His act of emancipated innocence thus sets the stage for integrity. Indeed, self-integrity presupposes emancipated innocence and particularly the ability to ignore social conventions. Although offered everything that society values—wealth and marriage to a Princess—the old man

91

rejects them, preferring to be true to himself. (A similar connection between integrity and emancipated innocence can be seen in the story of "The Magic Forest." Elves come to the old mother and together they laugh, sing, and dance. Emancipated by their magic, the old mother is able to step outside her troubles for a moment. Only then does she have a real choice, and only then can she authentically affirm her life just as it is. Conventional rationality would also tell her to forget her son, especially after he threw her out of the house, but she rejects that.)

Psychologically very astute, the present story goes on to add a further message about self-integrity which is not often appreciated. In the tale, the Princess, the King, and the Queen decide to visit the grasscutter. If the old man cares little about wealth, he still prides himself upon being an honorable man, and pride is the key word here. To be shamed before the Princess seems intolerable to him. The old man could easily give up wealth and luxury, because they do not really matter to him. He has lived without them for all his life, and could continue to do so. But he could not so easily put aside personal honor. Pride represents the last—and perhaps most secret and personal—of his desires. So here the story distinguishes self-integrity from pride. The point is important because the two are easy to confuse.

In reflecting on one's personal history, late in life, it is sometimes hard not to become consumed with regret, lamenting roads not taken, or friendships left behind. Indeed, Erikson explicitly argued that if the older individual fails to attain a sense of self-integrity, despair is the result. On the other hand, in reminiscing, it is easy to be smug about the past. Over the years, most adults achieve something they justly feel proud of, whether it is raising a family successfully, or founding a new business. In retrospect, it is easy to excuse past mistakes, and exaggerate successes. Taken to an extreme, this leads to conceit. The individual affirms his life as something virtuous, heroic, generous, and wonderful. Indeed, the longitudinal research from Harvard and Berkeley offers many examples of this myth-making process. Individuals may recall how wonderful a marriage "always was," although the records from 20 years earlier reveal tremendous marital discord; or a person may describe his career as a personal calling that he or she never questioned, although interviews from years before reveal constant vocational doubts.[3]

Self-integrity or despair are not the only outcomes in later life. Egocentric pride and conceit are equally possible and as dreadful as despair. Self-integrity thus requires a middle path, combining self-transcendence on one hand, and self-affirmation on the other. Our story vividly portrays the danger of pride. Fearful he would be shamed before the Princess, the old man resolves to kill himself. He fails, and in despair he collapses, effectively surrendering his pride. Like the demons the old woman encounters in "The Sparrow's Gift," the old man needs a dark and tragic crisis to root out his pride.

At this point angelic beings appear. Notice, however, that the angels appear *after* the old man's pride collapses. So the angels are actually the effect, not the cause, of his rescue. Our elder tale thus contrasts with stories of youth, where magical beings provide the *means* of escape, rather than the result or reward of an action.

The angels bestow upon the old man unbelievable wealth. By now, we know that material riches signify psychological wealth. So our story suggests that true self-integrity, purified of conceit, involves psychological riches—a new level of inner integration and wholeness in life. The situation here is similar to that in "The Dragon King of the Sea," where the Dragon King's opulent palace symbolized inner completeness and harmony. Self-integrity, the present story suggests, is such a state. The riches it produces are its own reward.

In the present tale, the old man's wealth comes from angelic beings, so we might suspect an important link between the old man's wealth and something divine or spiritual. Indeed, the palace and its gardens are so wondrous they recall the images of Paradise and the Garden of Eden, places of ultimate perfection and fulfillment. Our tale seems to hint here that the old man reclaims the divine innocence of Adam and Eve before their biblical fall. Emancipated innocence and ego-integrity relate somehow to spiritual completion. Exactly what this means is as yet unclear, but the next story explains it more fully.

12

The Six Statues

(from Japan)

nce upon a time, there lived a kind old man and woman who were very poor. One New Year's Eve, they found they had no money to buy rice cakes for the holiday. Then they remembered seven straw hats the old man had made some time before. "I shall go to the village to sell them," the old man said. So his wife put one of the hats on his head, and the other six on his shoulders, and off he went in the snow.

All that day the old man tried peddling his hats, but no one bought any. So late in the afternoon, he trudged up the snowy trail back to his house, wrapped in misery. On his way, he noticed six statues of gods, standing in the snow. They were the guardian deities of children and looked so cold and lonely that the old man paused. "I cannot leave you to shiver here!" he exclaimed, and so he gave each statue a straw hat, tying them carefully on the gods' heads. Then the old man returned home.

The old woman sighed when her husband told her he had no rice cakes. But she smiled when he described giving his hats to the six statues. "Imagine how happy they must be!" she exclaimed. Later that night, after a meagre New Year's Eve dinner, the old man and his wife went to bed.

At midnight, they were awakened by strange noises outside their house. "Who could that be?" the old man exclaimed. They listened and made out the sound of people singing.

At that moment, the door flew open, and a bag landed in the middle of their hut. It fell open, revealing the prettiest rice cakes the old man and his wife had ever seen, smelling sweet and fresh. And when they looked through their door, they saw six statues, each with a straw hat, bowing a New Year's greeting to them!

Summarized from "The New Year Gift from the Six Jizos" in M. Ohta, Japanese Folklore in English (Tokyo: Miraishi, 1955), and F. H. Mayer, Ancient Tales in Modern Japan (Bloomington, Ind.: Indiana University Press, 1985).

Reflections: The Return of Wonder

This story is short, sweet, and (we might also think) simple. But its simplicity is deceptive. The tale elaborates on the nature of emancipated innocence in a mischievous way.

First notice the manner in which the old man gives his straw hats to the six stone statues. He does not offer the hats to the gods merely to throw them away, the way one might give table scraps to the dogs, or worn-out clothes to the poor. Quite the contrary, the old man reverently ties the hats on the statues and talks with them. His actions are quite unexpected and seemingly irrational. After all, if he thought of selling the hats in the first place, he could keep them and try again later. Besides, what would people think if they saw him talking to the statues? The old man seems to have lost his reason—just like old man who danced with demons, and the grasscutter who gave the Princess his life savings. By ignoring pragmatic considerations, dispensing with social convention and honoring a spontaneous feeling of the heart, these characters illustrate emancipated innocence.

The story emphasizes the unique combination of childlike spontaneity and mature practicality that constitutes emancipated innocence. The old man, for example, gives his straw hats to the statues *after* he tries selling them in the village, not before. He is a practical man, not a fool. Indeed, the old man's trip to the village and back again offers a metaphor for a journey into practical, human society, and then beyond it. In this respect, the old man contrasts sharply with the typical hero or heroine in tales of youth. The young protagonist also gives away valuable belongings, but in a naive way, while still *on the way to a challenge.* The youth might, for instance, give a hungry animal his last piece of bread, out of generosity. But this magnanimity is naive. The youth assumes that everything will work out somehow, even though a terrible dragon lies before him. Or he thinks he can succeed in his ordeal without food or rest. His innocence is that of the child who has not yet gone into the world, struggled with it, and learned its many hard and humbling lessons. The old man in the present story, on the other hand, *has* been in the world, knows how to take care of himself, and has done so for many years. He knows his limits and those of the world, too. So our story is quite clear that emancipated innocence presupposes years of pragmatism.

The story adds a mischievous detail that underscores the theme of childlike innocence. The six statues are quite unique. They are not likenesses of the Goddess of Mercy or the Buddha, to whom adults were more likely to pray long ago in Japan. Our tale specifically—and playfully—says that the six statues are those of the guardian deities of *children!*

That night, the six statues come to life and visit the old man and his wife, bringing rice cakes as gifts. The six gods usher in a magical New Year for the old couple. Heart-warming and enchanting as it is, what might the symbolic meaning of the miraculous visit be? On one level, the event symbolizes rejuvenation. Cold, lifeless statues become living beings, suggesting that no matter how dreary or rigid life may seem, the chance for renewal remains. The setting of the story underscores the point—it is winter, a barren and colorless season often equated with old age. But the story also specifically says the events occur on New Year's Eve. As the last day of the year, New Year's Eve conjures up an image of decline and death. As the threshold of a new year, the day also points to new beginnings.

Yet the theme of inanimate objects coming to life occurs in other elder tales. A particularly charming one is the Cossack story of "The Straw Ox,"[1] where a poor old woman makes a straw ox, and her husband coats it with pitch to keep it together. She takes it to the field, treating it as if it were real, and the ox comes alive. Different forest animals approach the straw ox, and then become stuck to its tar. So the woman takes the animals home. Her husband spares their lives in return for their promise to help him and his wife. The forest animals bring honey, fruits, and vegetables, and the old couple live happily afterward. Appearing as it does all over the world, the theme of inanimate objects coming to life must be important. As usual, a good starting point for interpreting the motif is to construe the concrete event as a symbol for a psychological process.

Treating stone statues as if they were living people is *animism*. A good example of this attitude comes from children, who regard their teddy bears not simply as stuffed animals, but as real personalities. Animism is also the attitude that enlivens mythic consciousness[2] and accords souls to trees and rocks, no less than people. The ancient hunter apologized to his prey before killing it, because he believed the animal was conscious and had a spirit, just as he did. And the aboriginal woodcutter placates the tree he fells, speaking to it and making offerings, respecting it as a person. Nature is full of sprites, dryads, and nymphs in mythic consciousness.

As children grow up, they lose this animism and the material, scientific, pragmatic view of the world predominates, partly by necessity. Nature is measured and objectified, the better to manipulate it.[3] Solving problems preoccupies the adult, not talking with trees. What the present tale suggests is that the reclamation of animism and mythic awareness is a task for later life.

Early researchers in aging noted just such animism in later life. Older adults treat inanimate objects as if they were living things much more often than young adults do.[4] In addition, older individuals more frequently see magical qualities in events, and appeal to supernatural explanations, a finding that has been quantified using the Thematic Apperception Test.[5] This animism of older adults is usually interpreted as a regression in intellectual capacity, the loss of logical capacities. As we discussed before, however, a growing number of psychologists have recently challenged the simple regression model of aging.[6] This raises an important question: is there perhaps a mature form of animism and mythic consciousness? There is a precedent for this in emancipated innocence, which is the mature reclamation of childlike innocence.

Martin Buber, a 20th century philosopher, provides an affirmative, if theoretical, answer. What he calls the "You-attitude" is a mature form of animism.[7] This "You-attitude" is what we normally use with close friends and loved ones—we treat them with respect, affection and sensitivity. By contrast, we use what Buber calls an "It-attitude" for animals and objects, treating them as "its," or objects—things to be used. Of course, we sometimes apply the It-attitude to people, too, using them like common objects, but this is usually condemned. Indeed, the traditional ideal of universal love, or *agape*, is simply the You-attitude applied to all people. Buber argues that we can extend such love to animals and plants, too. We can apply the You-attitude to dogs and trees, no less than to friends and family. We then experience animals and objects as unique, irreplaceable individuals. The central element of this experience is wonder—an appreciation of mystery. For Buber, in fact, the You-attitude is almost a mystical experience.

The crucial question is whether this mature spirit of wonder and mystery occurs in real life. Empirical observations answer, "Yes." Numinous experiences, bordering on the mystical, seem to increase in the second half of life.[8] Such experiences can—and must—be distinguished from regressive, or pathological, experiences.[9] Statements from real people, however, are the most convincing evidence for a mature form of wonder. Flora Arnstein, a retired teacher, wrote the following poem in her 90's:

> That it can never be known
> Makes it all the more alluring,
> Enticing, too, so that one goes on trying.
> Every morning is an invitation,
> The sun friendly as an unafraid child,
> Each trifle enjoyable: the shoe-horn
> Emerging from the shoe-heel,
> The tooth-brush rinsed of paste;
> All small delectables: the brewing coffee,
> Even the charred toast,
> And the thrust of cool air

As one reaches the street.
This is no euphoria, just an aura
Of good feeling.[10]

In her verse a spirit of mythic delight emerges. She celebrates the present, very ordinary moment, apprehending the mystery and divinity in it. Wonder returns—the marvel a child might feel when first encountering toothpaste or coffee. And the greatest magic is that this delight returns on the ten thousandth time around.

The return of mythic experience often takes the form of delight in nature. One woman in her 60's, for instance, consulted me about her husband, who suffered from Alzheimer's disease. Despite the stresses of attending to him, she was still able to enjoy life. As she described her experience: "I take walks every morning, rain or shine, and I love it. The world seems so fresh. Everything is alive—the trees, the birds, the water on the lake!" For others, wonder returns in becoming a grandparent. As one woman described her reaction upon beholding her grandchild for the first time: "It was a wonder, a mystery, and there was something else, too—a wonder at nature. It was a spiritual or religious experience. You know, just as if you would sit there and look at a flower for a long time—that kind of feeling, a religious feeling."[11]

Individuals, and particularly men, shift away from a future-oriented preoccupation with achieving things to an enjoyment of the present moment. A new sensuousness emerges, an aestheticism that often surprises individuals who have devoted many years to purely pragmatic pursuits.[12] Romano Guardini, a philosopher, described his experience, writing when he was 70:

Existence now takes on the character, we might say, of a still-life in a Cezanne. There is a table. Upon the table, a plate. Upon the plate, some apples. Nothing else. Everything is there, clear and evident. Nothing left to ask or to answer. And yet mystery everywhere. There is more in these things than meets the eye: more than the simple individuality of each thing. . . . It might even be that mystery is the very stuff of being: things, events, everything that happens and which we call life.[13]

Central to this attitude of wonder is the individual's affirmation of life just as it is in the present. The person neither hankers after a lost past, nor yearns for a future yet to be.[14] Here we come to a close connection between restoring a spirit of wonder in life and the development of self-integrity. As mentioned earlier, integrity is an affirmation of one's life just as one lived it, for better or worse. Self-integrity is thus an affirmation of one's *past*. The return of wonder involves a similar affirmation of the *present*, down to its small, ordinary events. The return of wonder is an extension and deepening of self-integrity.[15]

The connection between the two attitudes can be seen in a statement by the psychoanalyst Martin Grotjahn, writing in the last years of his life:

I don't work anymore, I don't walk anymore. Peculiarly enough, I feel well about it . . .

I sit in the sun watching the falling leaves slowly sail across the waters of the swimming pool. I think, I dream, I draw, I sit—I feel free of worry—almost free of this world of reality.

If anyone had told me that I would be quietly happy just sitting here, reading a little, writing a little, and enjoying life in a quiet and modest way, I, of course, would not have believed. That a walk across the street to the corner of the park satisfies me when I always thought a four hour walk was just not good enough: that surprises me.[16]

A quiet, delightful sort of magic animates Grotjahn's experience. The world comes to life in a tranquil way, and even small events become filled with mystery and wonder. Grotjahn affirms his life in its simplicity and naturalness. Doing something noteworthy or reaching for a distant goal, like four hours of walking, matters less now. The ambitions of youth are replaced by a mature delight in the present.

Our story does not end with the return of mythic experience, however. It is an unusually deep tale, and specifically says that the six statues are of *deities*. So the story hints at a connection between emancipated innocence and something divine. It is not a magician or a fairy godmother that comes to the old couple, but six *gods*. And what the gods give to the old couple are rice cakes, which are ritual foods in Japan, customarily offered at shrines to the gods or to ancestors. So the rice cakes are analogous to the Christian Eucharist or the Jewish Passover meal: the statues give the old couple spiritual sustenance, not just food. The magic here is not merely wish-fulfillment—a hungry man's dream of free food. The connection between emancipated innocence and the sacred also occurs in "The Simple Grasscutter," where angels appear at the end of the story and bestow fabulous wealth upon the old man in a scene reminiscent of Heaven and Paradise.

Indeed, the attitude of wonder and emancipated innocence is a state of mind that resembles what many religious traditions call "enlightenment."[17] According to diverse schools, a key element of enlightenment is the apprehension of the world in its wonder and mystery, just as it is. A poem from a Zen Buddhist scholar highlights the similarity of spiritual enlightenment to the late-life experience of mystery:

> *Silently a flower blooms,*
> *In silence it falls away;*
> *Yet here now, at this moment, at this place,*
> *the whole of the flower, the whole of*
> *the world is blooming.*
> *This is the talk of the flower, the truth of the blossom.*
> *The glory of eternal life is fully shining here.*[18]

This Zen poem is strikingly similar to the verse by Flora Arnstein, and the comments by Martin Grotjahn and Romano Guardini. Kindred accounts of spiritual illumination come from Christianity, Judaism, and Hinduism.[19] Together they suggest that spiritual enlightenment and emancipated innocence involve a mature form of mythic experience.

Spiritual illumination is surely not common, and in general, the higher the phase of development, the rarer it is.[20] Dwelling on the connection between spiritual illumination and late-life development may thus seem abstract and impractical. But my purpose is to emphasize what *can* happen in the second half of life, not what *customarily* occurs. And this, indeed, is the function of elder tales: to portray the highest measure of humanity, not a conventional one—an ideal to strive toward, rather than an average to settle for.

"The Old Man Who Lost His Wen," "The Simple Grasscutter," and "The Six Statues" have a single message. They suggest that the return of magic in the second half of life can take the form of mythic consciousness and spiritual illumination. Enlightenment can be a crowning virtue of maturity.

13

The Widow and the Frog

(from Tibet)

nce upon a time, an old widow lived alone in a small hut. One day, she went to draw water from the stream, and a large frog hopped up to her. The frog opened its mouth and asked, "Dear lady, will you be my mother?"

The widow was shocked to hear a frog speak. "I cannot be your mother," she stammered fearfully, "you are a frog, and I am human!" With that she hurried away, thinking the frog was really a demon.

The next day, as the old woman sat drinking her tea, she felt as if somebody was watching her. When she looked out the window of her hut, she saw the large frog staring at her. "Please, dear lady," the frog asked again, "will you be my mother?"

His eyes were so big and sad that the old woman felt moved. "But how could I be your mother?" the old widow asked. "You are a frog, and I am human! Where would you sleep, and what would you eat?"

"I would sleep on the grate of the stove," the frog replied, "and I would eat what you eat! Are we not all the same, under the skin?"

The old widow hurried away, thinking the frog was trying to enchant her. The next day, when she went to draw water from the stream, she saw the frog sitting there, look-ing very sad and lonely. "Dear lady," the frog asked again, "will you be my mother?"

The old woman sighed. How could she turn down the poor creature? She herself knew the meaning of loneliness. "Very well," she said, "I will be your mother!" The frog croaked with joy and jumped high into the air. That day, it moved into the old woman's hut and that night it slept on the grate of the stove. "Strange," the old woman mused, "I thought frogs like cool damp places, not warm, dry ones!"

The next morning, the old woman cooked some barley gruel. It was all she had because she was so poor. So the frog said he was going to find some cheese for her. And off he hopped to the market. The frog was gone all day, and the old widow began to worry. "He is so small!" she fretted, "some-one could step on him!" Later that day, a mule walked into the yard, loaded down with cheese. And on the mule sat the frog.

The frog explained that he had gone to the market, and waited for several hours. When a cheese merchant walked by, the frog jumped on his mule and proceeded to ride around the market. Everybody was astonished to see the frog driving the mule, and ran away. So the frog returned home with the cheese.

The next day, the frog announced that he would seek a bride for himself. "But how will you find a frog who can talk?" the widow asked.

"Frog?" the frog laughed. "I don't need a frog! I am going to the village for my bride!" And off he hopped.

Later that day, the frog returned. He announced that he was marrying the daughter of the village merchant. The old woman was astonished because she knew how proud the merchant was, and his wife, too, because their daughter was the most beautiful maiden of the village. So the frog explained that he had asked the merchant for the maiden's

106

hand. "When he refused," the frog said, "I coughed and he changed his mind."

"You coughed?" the widow exclaimed.

"Yes," the frog said, and he coughed. A great wind arose, and blew away the roof of the widow's hut.

"I see, I see!" she exclaimed. So the frog smiled, and instantly, the wind vanished, and the roof reappeared, as if nothing had happened.

"Then I asked the merchant's wife," the frog continued, "and when she refused, I wept."

"You wept?" the widow asked, and so the frog cried. Water flooded the house and threatened to wash everything away. "I see, I see!" the widow exclaimed. The frog smiled, and the water vanished, restoring everything.

"Finally," he said, "I asked the daughter, and when she refused, I laughed." Then the frog laughed, and fire appeared everywhere, burning the old widow's home.

"I see, I see!" the widow cried out. The frog smiled, the flames vanished, and everything was restored as before.

The next day, the frog's bride arrived. She was fearful of becoming the wife of a frog, but when she met the old widow, she felt more at ease. So she soon settled into her new life. A few days later, a great tournament of horse racing was held near the village, and the old widow, the frog, and his wife decided to attend. Just as they left for the tournament, though, the frog remembered that he had not fed the animals in the barn. So he turned back, and the old widow and the young wife watched the races alone. That day, all the contests were won by a mysterious young man whom nobody recognized. So the old widow and the young wife hurried home to tell the frog about the unknown champion. The frog was sorry he missed the excitement, so they all decided to attend the next day's events.

The following morning, the three started out for the tournament, but the frog remembered he had neglected to water the animals. So he hopped back home, and the two women went on to the races alone. Like the day before, the mysterious horseman won all the races. By this time, the old widow and the young wife were beginning to wonder about their frog.

The next day, they all started off for the races again, but the frog once more remembered a chore he had left undone, and returned home. This time, the widow and the wife secretly followed him. When they arrived at the house, the frog was nowhere to be seen, but there was a suit of frog skin, hung up neatly behind the door. The young wife quickly took the suit and burned it. At that moment, a young man came in the door, and it was none other than the mysterious champion. He saw the suit burning and rushed to retrieve it. "What are you doing!" he cried out, but the suit vanished in the flames.

"I am a magic being," he explained later to his wife and mother. But from then on, he stayed in his human form. His wife was delighted, his mother was proud, and the three lived happily together. "After all," the former frog said, "are we not the same under the skin?"

Summarized from "The Frog" in F. and A. Hyde-Chambers, Tibetan Folk Tales (Boulder, Colo.: Shambhala, 1981); by arrangement with Shambhala Publications, 300 Massachusetts Ave., Boston, MA 02115. A similar tale can be found in F. H. Mayer, Ancient Tales in Modern Japan (Bloomington, Ind.: Indiana University Press, 1985).

Reflections: Mediation and Transcendence

The plot of this fairy tale will be familiar to most readers as, basically, the story of the frog-prince. The present tale is unique in involving an old widow, but that small difference symbolizes an important new task for the second half of life—the elder's role in society.

The first thing to notice is that the story falls naturally into two parts. The first half focuses on the old widow, and her reactions to meeting the frog, while the second half focuses on the frog

108

and his adventures. The tale begins with the usual theme of loss—
the old woman is a widow and poor. Then magic appears unexpectedly in her life, in the form of a talking frog. From the outset, it
is clear that the frog is a central symbol. One possible interpretation is that the frog represents some part of the old woman's personality. We saw an example of this symbolism in the story of
"The Dragon King," where a little boy led the old fisherman into
the ocean, symbolizing the task of reclaiming the innocence of
childhood in later life.

In the present tale, the frog is clearly male and turns out to be
a great horseman, so he makes a good symbol for the old woman's
masculine side. As discussed before, women often suppress their
assertiveness and independence in the first half of life because of
social pressures. After mid-life, these neglected masculine traits
emerge from the unconscious, and the task for the mature woman
is to integrate them into her life. The story symbolizes the process
in a charming way: the frog hops out of a stream and approaches
the widow. Like the ocean, streams often symbolize the unconscious, although in a less dramatic way. Since Tibet is the source
of this tale, and is far from any ocean, the story depicts a stream. In
using a frog, the tale also adds a nice touch. Frogs begin life as
tadpoles—aquatic creatures—and then develop into land animals.
Their movement from water to land symbolizes the transition
from unconsciousness to consciousness, a symbolism noted by
both mythologists and psychoanalysts alike.[1]

The frog is not just a symbol of the old woman's suppressed
masculinity, however, because his magic is clearly extraordinary.
In wooing the merchant's daughter, the frog coughs, weeps, and
laughs, and his actions produce a terrible wind, a horrible flood,
and a disastrous fire. The frog controls wind, fire, and water, and
this is deeply symbolic. In many mythologies around the world,
the four basic elements of the world are earth, air, fire, and water,
and Tibetan folklore is no exception. If the frog controls these fundamental constituents of the world, he must be divine or magical,
which our story confirms at the end. In accepting the frog into her
life, then, the widow not only recovers her masculine side, but also
makes contact with a numinous or supernatural reality. This
brings up an important task discussed before—transcending the

109

conscious self to embrace noble visions of God, Society, or the inner Self.

Notice that the widow invites the frog into her life out of a sense of compassion—she thinks about how lonely the frog must be and worries about his welfare. This is the spirit of generativity, and an example of self-transcendence. The importance of this theme can be seen if we compare the present story with a youth tale from the Grimms' collection, "The Frog King." In the German story, a *young* princess accidentally drops a golden ball into a well. A frog hops out and promises to retrieve the ball, but only if she will let him eat with her at the dinner table. To regain her toy, the princess agrees. She makes contact with the magic frog out of self-interest, not self-transcendence. When the widow adopts the frog as her son, her action also is outrageous, violating social conventions and rational thinking. The event recalls the old man who danced with demons, and the one who gave his hats to the six statues. The story thus alludes to the theme of emancipated innocence.

So far, the story has recapitulated the major themes in elder tales, from loss to the return of magic, on to self-transcendence and generativity, moving finally to emancipated innocence. But this is only the first half of the tale! The story quickly goes on to describe how the frog finds a bride, marries her, and eventually reveals his true identity. He starts a life of his own, quite independent of the old widow. The story thus suggests that we cannot interpret the frog just as a symbol of the old widow's masculinity and spirituality. He is also a person in his own right. Indeed, as a young husband with a young wife, the frog makes a good symbol for youth in general. I suggest therefore that the relationship between the widow and the frog symbolizes the ideal role the elder plays with respect to youth. And this is the new theme upon which the story focuses.

Here other details become important. Although the magic frog controls fire, air, and water, he apparently does not control earth—the fourth mythic element. But earth also makes a good symbol for the earthly realm, the material world, secular society, and practical reality. And this is the domain the widow has mastered in her many years of life. (Worldly wisdom, as previously discussed, is the province of mature adults.) Although the frog is a magic being, he is still apparently helpless in earthly matters until the widow adopts him. He needs her, despite his powers. The same theme appears in many other elder tales, like the Arabian story of "The Enchanted Head," or the Japanese tale of "Princess Moonlight."[2] In these stories, a magical or divine youth requires the help of an older person in order to get on in life. And what the elder provides is practical skill and worldly knowledge.

Elder tales are psychologically perceptive here. Young men and women are often caught up in noble visions, grand ideals, and dramatic intimacies. They have plenty of energy, enthusiasm, and emotion, which are well symbolized by fire, air, and water. What they lack is practical grounding—the earth element—and that is precisely what the mature adult offers: discipline, knowledge and patience, the pragmatic virtues that help make enthusiasm productive, and wild emotions tolerable. We saw something of this theme in the tale of "The Old Alchemist," where the old father used his wisdom to channel his son-in-law's quixotic ambitions, transforming the young man's dreams into a practical venture. The present story demonstrates a similar process. Through the widow, the young frog-man becomes human, finds a home, a wife, and finally, some recognition in society.

The story thus portrays an important task for the mature adult—to mediate between transcendent visions and mundane realities for the benefit of youth. The elder does this not by forcing practical necessities on the youth, but by providing a *model*. Ideally the elder reexperiences his or her own transcendent ideals from youth, and then integrates them with worldly experience, offering advice and example.

Such a mediating role for elders can be found in cultures around the world.[3] In hunter-gatherer tribes and in agricultural societies, the elder is the guardian of sacred secrets. Old men preside over the initiation of boys into manhood, and old women over that of girls, passing on the sacred traditions of the culture. But at the same time, elders also teach vital practical knowledge—secrets of hunting, weaving, foretelling weather, and so forth. If elders intercede with the world beyond, placating gods and the spirits of the dead, they also train youth for this world. To use the words of David Gutmann, a social gerontologist, elders are "bridgeheads to the sacred."[4] They link youth to transcendent realities *and* practical realities.

Although the importance of elders has diminished greatly in industrialized societies, the archetypal role remains. In his in-depth interviews with older individuals, for instance, the gerontologist John Kotre has found that many describe trying to embody ideals and traditions for the younger generation.[5] They struggle to be living models for youth—and young men and women respond. Many youths, for instance, have joined the religious order founded by Mother Theresa. Working tirelessly with the most wretched of India's poor, Mother Theresa personifies an inspiring ideal of saintly love. But more importantly, she embodies *dedication*—the integration of inspiration with practical work. Through her order, she helps young women transform their own spiritual inspirations into useful practice.

Grandparents often play a similar, if less dramatic, role with their grandchildren, something true in cultures around the world.[6] Indeed, many successful individuals cite their grandparents, more than their parents,[7] as inspiring personal models. The French philosopher, Jean-Paul Sartre, for instance, remembers his grandfather with great fondness, respect, and inspiration. And Margaret Mead, the pioneering American anthropologist, recalls the formative influence of her grandparents in her childhood. To the child, the grandparent often seems larger than life, heroic and wise, and yet accessible at the same time—at once awe-inspiring and familiar, magical yet human. And this is the essence of the mediating role, combining transcendent ideals with everyday reality.

The elder's role also extends into mentoring. Ideally, the mentor does not merely pass on practical skills to an apprentice. The mentor also conveys ethical ideals which give meaning, honor, and discipline to practice. Senior physicians and jurists, for instance, often point out how technical expertise is not enough in learning medicine or law. The young professional must also develop an ethical sense, ultimately rooted in a tradition of healing or justice. Without such an idealistic context, the youth may abuse his new knowledge for selfish aims.[8] Transcendent inspiration must be integrated with worldly abilities.

A real-life example is perhaps the best way to illustrate the developmental importance of the mediating role. Mr. J, a successful businessman, came to therapy in his 60's for depression. Shortly afterward, he began having sudden moments of inspiration, quite out of character with his usual phlegmatic self. Events like hearing the national anthem sung at a baseball game or attending a political rally moved him to tears. At those times, Mr. J felt a part of the American drama, inspired by a spirit of patriotism he had not known since youth. He was terribly embarrassed by his feelings, and at first thought they only represented foolish sentimentality. Indeed, he suppressed his reactions so his wife would not see the tears in his eyes. Slowly, however, Mr. J came to accept his inspirations as valid and important, and he began recalling the ideals he had entertained as a youth, and which he had put aside in his long business career. Partly in response to these experiences, he left his successful career in business and turned to consulting and teaching. He made a special effort to foster the careers of younger men and women. "This way," he explained, "I can do my part for the American dream!"

Like the old widow in our story, who accepted the frog only after much hesitation, Mr. J embraced his resurgent ideals only with embarrassment and reluctance. And just as the old woman finally became a mother to the frog, Mr. J integrated his renewed idealism into his life by becoming a mentor to young men and women. He grounded his feelings of inspiration in concrete and altruistic ways, and avoided falling victim to mere sentimentality. In essence, Mr. J mediated between personal inspiration—his vision of the American dream—and the practical needs of young entrepreneurs, for the benefit of society.

The story of "The Widow and the Frog" also reflects an important insight about the mediating role: it does not fall upon just any old person, but to an elder who has grown and wizened over the years. Indeed, cultures around the world distinguish between the *elder* and the *elderly,* those who learn to mediate with transcendent truths and those who merely deteriorate with age.[9] Our story conveys this point in a subtle way, by introducing the mediating role *after* alluding to poverty, self-transcendence, and emancipated innocence. This suggests that the mediating role is a developmental achievement, and not merely an inevitable effect of aging—a challenge and a task, not merely the accumulation of years.

The Fisherman and the Djinn

(from Arabia)

ong ago and far away, an old fisherman lived with his wife by the sea. Each day the old man cast his net four times, no more and no less, earning his livelihood from what he drew up from the sea. One day bad luck plagued him. The first time he cast his net, he hauled up a dead jackass, the second time, only an urn full of sand, and the third time, only potsherds. In despair, the old man prayed to Allah, asking for better luck on his last attempt. And sure enough, when he retrieved his net, he found a small copper bottle entangled in it.

The flask was sealed and holy scriptures were written on its stopper. Out of curiosity, the old man opened the bottle. He found nothing in it but a moment later, smoke poured from the flask, and a hideous djinn materialized. The monster bowed to the fisherman, and said, "Mighty Solomon, I salute you and thank you for releasing me from my prison!"

The fisherman shook with terror. "I am not Solomon," he said, "the great king has been dead a thousand years!"

The djinn paused and then laughed. "In that case, prepare to die, little man!"

The fisherman was horrified. "But I freed you from the flask!" he cried out. "What gratitude is this?"

"Solomon imprisoned me in this bottle, because I

rebelled against him," the djinn explained, "and so for the first hundred years, I vowed that whomever released me I would make rich beyond all dreams. But no one came. In the next hundred years, I promised that I would grant three wishes to my liberator. But still no one came. So I became angry, and I swore a great oath that I would slay the man who freed me, on the spot. Now prepare to die, mortal!"

The fisherman pleaded for his life, but to no avail. So he thought quickly, and finally said, "Very well, you can kill me, you ingrateful monster! But in the Most Terrible Name of Allah, at least tell me the truth." The djinn trembled to hear the Name. "How could a great djinn like you fit in such a small bottle?" the fisherman demanded. "You must have come from elsewhere."

The djinn felt insulted. "Foolish man," he roared, "you disbelieve me? I shall show you my magic power and then I shall kill you!" With that the djinn turned into a cloud of smoke, and poured back into the flask. Instantly, the old fisherman stopped up the bottle.

A tiny voice came from the flask. "Let me out!" the djinn screamed.

"Never!" the fisherman said.

So the djinn spoke more gently. "I will reward you richly!" the djinn promised, "if you release me."

"You are a murderer," the fisherman replied, "and I shall throw your bottle into the sea and build my house on this spot to warn people never to fish here."

"No, no!" the djinn cried out. "I was only testing you! Now that I know you are a man who fears Allah, I will reward you!"

"You take me for a fool," the fisherman laughed. He lit his pipe, sat on the sand and then smiled. "This reminds me of the story of the 'Ungrateful King,' " the old man mused.

"I have not heard that tale," the djinn said. "Please tell it to me! But I cannot hear well in this bottle, so you must open the stopper first."

116

"I shall not release you," the fisherman laughed, "but I shall tell you the tale." And so he recounted the story of a King who fell ill with a horrible disease, worse than leprosy. None of his physicians and magicians could cure him, until one day a doctor came by, who recognized the ailment. The physician cured the King, and in gratitude the monarch honored the doctor above all other men in the land. This made the Vizier jealous, so he whispered to the King about how easily the doctor could poison the monarch. The foolish King heeded his Vizier's lies and threw the doctor into prison. All the good man's pleas were fruitless and the King put the doctor to death. Just before he died, the physician mentioned a magic book he possessed which contained all the knowledge of the world. So the King took the dead man's book, and looked through it, only to find that the volume had no writing. Instead, its pages were poisoned, and soon afterward the King died in agony. "Just so," the fisherman concluded, "Allah would have taken vengeance on you if you had killed me!"

"But our situation is not like that story at all," the djinn protested. "It is more like the tale of 'The Prince and the Ogre.'"

"Ah," the fisherman murmured, "I have not heard that one. Tell it to me."

"I cannot remember it from in this bottle," the djinn said, "release me and I am sure I will recall it better."

"Perhaps another thousand years at the bottom of the sea would help your memory?" the fisherman asked.

"No, no," the djinn said, "I remember the story now." And so he told his tale and a marvellous one it was, too. When the djinn was through, the fisherman smiled.

"That was a good story," he said, "but not as good as this one. . . ." And so the two spent the afternoon telling stories, until the fisherman noted the late hour. "I must leave soon, my friend," he told the djinn.

"Please release me!" the djinn asked again. "I vow I will

117

not harm you, and I promise I will help you. On the Most Terrible Name, I swear!" The flask shook as the djinn trembled inside.

The fisherman paused, and then said, "Very well, I will release you."

The old man took off the stopper, and the djinn reappeared. Instantly, the djinn kicked the bottle into the sea. "Remember your oath!" the fisherman stuttered, his knees starting to knock.

The djinn scowled. Then he said gruffly, "Follow me."

The djinn took the old man deep into the wilderness and stopped at a beautiful lake, surrounded by four mountains. In the water swam fishes of four colors—red, yellow, blue, and white. "Throw your net here," the djinn told the old man, "but only once each day. And then take what you catch to the Sultan." With that, the djinn stamped his foot on the ground, the earth opened up, and the djinn vanished.

The fisherman threw his net in the lake, and immediately caught four fish, each a different color. They were more beautiful than anything he had seen, so the fisherman hurried to the Sultan's palace, and gave the fish to the monarch. The Sultan was astonished at the splendor of the fish, and rewarded the old man handsomely. Then the monarch gave the fish to a cook to fry. When the cook put the creatures on the stove, the wall of the kitchen burst asunder, and a woman stepped out. "Have you been faithful to your covenants?" she asked the fish. All the creatures replied, "Yes," and the woman and the fish vanished.

The cook told the Sultan what had happened, but he did not believe it. So he asked the fisherman to bring four more fish the next day and the old man did. But the same thing happened: just as the cook was about to fry the fish, a woman appeared out of the wall, talked to the creatures, and then disappeared with them. The Sultan decided to see this strange event himself, so he asked the fisherman to bring four more fish, and the old man obliged again. This time the

Sultan watched as the cook prepared to fry the fish. The wall split asunder and a black man appeared, asking the fish, "Have you been faithful to your covenants?" The fish all answered, "Yes," and then vanished with the stranger.

"There is magic here!" the Sultan said. So he summoned the fisherman to the palace and asked, "Where do you catch your fish?" The old man led the Sultan to the lake surrounded by four mountains. "I think," the Sultan said thoughtfully, "I shall explore this area myself."

That night the Sultan hiked deep into the mountains and came at length upon a dark castle. He ventured into the gloomy place, but not a soul stirred there. Then he heard someone moaning and followed the sound to a young man writhing in pain, his waist and legs turned into stone!

"Allah have mercy!" the Sultan exclaimed, "what happened to you?" The youth was astonished to see a human face in the enchanted castle, but he quickly poured out his story of woe. He was the Prince of the Western Islands, he explained, and had married a beautiful woman. But his wife turned out to be a dreadful sorceress, and worse, she loved another man. When he discovered their ungodly affair, the Prince said, he drew his sword and struck the evil man. In revenge, the sorceress turned him half into stone, and cast a spell upon the whole land. His islands became mountains, the sea, a desert, and his beloved people, fish in the lake— ruby, yellow, blue, and white, for the four faiths of his realm. Each night, the hapless Prince reported, the sorceress came to him and flogged him. Elsewhere in the palace lay the witch's lover, neither dying nor recovering from his wound. "You must leave quickly," the Prince concluded, "before the witch finds you here!"

"No," the Sultan replied, "I will help you if I can." The Sultan pondered the situation and came up with a plan. He searched through the castle until he discovered the witch's lover half asleep in a dark room. The evil man mistook the Sultan for the sorceress and whispered for a few minutes.

The Sultan listened intently, and then slew the wretch, cast the vile body aside, and crawled in the bed himself, drawing the curtains around him. In a few minutes, the witch appeared.

The Sultan feigned the voice of the witch's lover. "Dear heart," he said to the witch, "while I slept just now, I dreamed about why I do not recover from my wound. It is because each night you torment the young man, and I cannot be healed until you free him!"

The evil woman rejoiced and rushed to the youth to release him from her spell. Then she returned to her beloved. The Sultan whispered in a louder voice. "I feel strength returning to me, but I am not yet healed. The people you changed into fish cry out each night to Allah and he will not free me of my affliction until you free them of theirs!"

The witch hastened to the lake. She uttered magic words, and in an instant, the mountains became islands, the desert a sea, the lake a city, and from the fish sprang all the people of the land. The witch rushed back to her beloved, and the Sultan killed her.

In the next moment, the gloomy castle became a palace full of fountains and flowers. The Prince and all his court rushed in to thank the Sultan for liberating them and they sang praises of his courage and cleverness. But the Sultan was a fair and honest man, so he sent for the old fisherman. "This is the man we should honor," he declared. The Sultan had no wife, and when he met the fisherman's eldest daughter, he fell in love with her and married her, making her Queen. Then the Prince met the fisherman's younger daughter, and he fell in love with her and married her. Finally the Sultan bestowed upon the fisherman a robe of honor and fabulous riches. "You never have to go fishing again," the Sultan declared. And so the old man and his wife spent the rest of their days in comfort and honor. But the old man often went fishing anyway—just for old time's sake.

Summarized from "The Fisherman and the Djinn," in R. Burton, trans., Tales from the Arabian Nights (New York: Avenel, 1978).

Reflections: Mediation and the Emancipation of Society

The story of "The Fisherman and the Djinn" is an extraordinarily rich one. It reintroduces many of the themes discussed up till now, and adds a new one. In the process, the story reveals how all the themes in elder tales fit together. Most stories dramatize one or two motifs, and like pieces of a mosaic, each tale constitutes only a fragment of a larger picture. A few stories, like the present one, depict almost all the themes, and thus reveal the underlying drama of elder tales—the saga of the second half of life. Even more important, the present story tells us why elder tales have become so fragmented and unfamiliar in modern culture. In essence, "The Fisherman and the Djinn" reveals the tale of elder tales themselves.

The story starts out with an old fisherman who is, of course, quite poor. On a particularly bad day, struggle as he may, he brings up only rubbish in his net. Two aspects of this opening scenario leap out. First are the elements of poverty and loss, which are the usual setting of elder tales. And second, the old man lives by the seashore, between land and sea. As previously noted, this location symbolizes the boundary between consciousness and unconsciousness, and alludes to a major task for the second half of life—reclaiming what was neglected or repressed in youth. And that is precisely what starts the tale: after several discouraging incidents,[1] the old man fishes up a magic bottle and opens it.

The djinn that materializes from the flask threatens to kill the fisherman, so great is the spirit's anger over his imprisonment. The djinn thus provides a dramatic symbol of repressed anger, festering until it bursts out as rage. In the fisherman's confrontation with the monster, the story raises a common theme in elder tales—the encounter with one's own evil. The old woman who cut the sparrow's tongue off, recall, had a similar meeting with demons.

However, the symbolism of the djinn runs deeper in the

121

present story. The djinn was imprisoned by Solomon, centuries before the fisherman appeared on the scene. By referring to ancient times and supernatural abilities, the djinn reveals his numinous nature. He does not just symbolize the old man's repressed rage, but the entire supernatural realm. This is the theme of a transcendent encounter, which we witnessed in "An Old Mother's Sorrow," and "The Dragon King." In the present tale, the djinn is horrifying rather than helpful or inspiring, and it is natural to ask why the djinn is so terrible. The story makes clear, after all, that the fisherman does not deserve punishment. The writings of Rudolph Otto, a German theologian, offer a possible interpretation. He observed that transcendent experiences typically evoke a mixture of fascination, mystery, and *horror*.[2] It is no accident that we refer to the *fear* of God, as much as to a fear of ghosts and goblins. The two are intimately connected. Transcendent insights are not just beautiful and heavenly. They can also be overwhelming. Indeed, this is a major reason that people are able to embrace numinous experiences in late life, when they could not tolerate them in youth: maturity and experience strengthen the individual, allowing one to withstand both the ecstatic and horrifying dimensions of transcendent revelations.

Faced with the djinn, the old man seems doomed, and he manages to save himself only by tricking the spirit back into the bottle. The fisherman's escape depends upon his insight into the psychology of vanity, and the djinn is quite vain. So our story raises the theme of wisdom as deceit combined with insight which we saw in "The Old Alchemist" and "The Wise Merchant."

After getting the djinn safely back in the bottle, the old fisherman does something remarkable. He sits down and converses with the djinn. He talks calmly with the monster who had vowed to kill him only moments before. What can we make of this odd conversation? The rational and conventional thing for the old man to do is to throw the flask back into the sea. After all, who knows what the djinn can do even from within the bottle? The next event is therefore dumbfounding. The djinn promises he will not harm the fisherman, the old man muses a while, and then releases the djinn. This seems to be a foolish act and even the fisherman is frightened when the djinn reappears in his awful majesty. The old man's decision nevertheless comes from the heart. It is spontaneous *and* reflective, and this brings us to the theme of emancipated innocence. Indeed, the present story is strikingly similar to that of "The Old Man Who Lost His Wen." Both men face horrifying demonic beings, and then, after due deliberation—but contrary to all reason—they put their lives in the hands of the monsters.

Notice that the fisherman and the djinn do not talk in an ordinary way. They exchange fairy tales. The detail might easily be overlooked, but it is quite insightful. The fisherman and the djinn use parables and metaphors to communicate with each other. They invoke the medium of image rather than logic, and of myth rather than reason. Far from being a simple-minded or child-like way of communication, parables offer a richer medium in which to communicate. Metaphors engage emotions and intuitions—the heart and soul, if you will. Indeed, most traditional religions recognize the power of metaphor and use "teaching tales" to make their points. Besides the Ten Commandments, the Bible has many striking parables.

Since the fisherman is an old man and the djinn is even older, we might wonder if the use of parables develops in the second half of life. Recent research on aging supports this suggestion.[3] With maturity, adults begin to understand metaphors in more complex ways, whether in proverbs or parables. For example, given the proverb, "Don't burn a candle at both ends," a young adult might say it means, "Don't do too many things at once," and leave it at that. An older adult more typically goes on to add, "But sometimes you have to, like if you're committed to your family *and* your work. I remember struggling with this when I first got married. It was hard, but it had to be done, despite what the proverb might say!" With greater life experience, the mature adult perceives many more connections between proverbs and real life, and apprehends more complex psychological truths.

The same process of enriched interpretation applies to parables. A story that was merely an amusing folktale when first heard in youth often becomes a profoundly meaningful metaphor later in life. John Kotre cites several dramatic examples from individuals he interviewed in his study.[4] One woman, for instance, was fascinated as a child by the tale of Bluebeard. She was struck then chiefly by the moral of the tale—the importance of resisting sexual temptation. By the age of 55, however, she realized there was

123

much more meaning in the tale. The story was in fact her life-script: she had been "butchered" by the men in her life, who acted the part of Bluebeard. With that searing insight and the help of therapy, she was able to start anew, altering her "script." The tale was no longer merely a story, but the summary of all her life experiences.

In the tale, the djinn then leads the old man to a secret lake. Surrounded by four mountains, and containing four kinds of fish in the four primary colors, the lake is obviously no ordinary one. Indeed, it has the features of a mandala, a symmetric geometrical symbol which represents numinous wholeness in myths and dreams. As Jung discussed at length,[5] mandalas often symbolize the higher or inner Self. So the magical lake is equivalent to the palace of the Dragon King in the earlier tale—both represent a supramundane realm of psychological wholeness.

The djinn then tells the old man to fish in the lake and take what he catches to the Sultan of the country. The old man does so and thereby assumes the role of go-between, mediating between the numinous world symbolized by the magic lake, and the mundane order personified by the younger Sultan. So the story conveys yet another theme of elder tales—mediation with the supernatural. Like the old woman in "The Widow and the Frog," the fisherman provides a critical link between the human and the superhuman, between a younger protagonist and a transcendent reality.

Notice the subtle switch in the kind of mediation the fisherman carries out. Initially the fisherman mediates with the djinn, telling stories to the creature. If we interpret the djinn at this point as a symbol for unconscious feelings like anger, the old man's mediation is personal and introspective. When the fisherman goes to the Sultan, the role changes: he now mediates between secular society and the divine order, and his role is no longer merely psychological, but social and spiritual. The same switch occurs in "The Widow and the Frog." In the first half of the story, the frog symbolizes the masculine side of the old woman and the old widow's relationship to the frog represents an introspective process in which she comes to terms with forgotten aspects of her personality. But in the second half, the frog emerges more clearly as an independent being—a young man with his own wife. He represents youth in general and the widow's relationship to him becomes a social one. She mediates between a transcendent realm and the secular order, helping the young frog to make the transition from one to the other.

The lesson here is often overlooked. Many psychologists of aging, Jung included, have emphasized the importance of introspection.[6] Indeed, many tasks portrayed in elder tales require introversion—coming to terms with one's own evil, or reclaiming the inner child, for example. However the present story, like "The Widow and the Frog," emphasizes that introspection is only a prelude to another task—mediating between secular society and transcendent truth, ultimately helping the next generation. Indeed, the most challenging task of later life can be said to be uniting inner exploration and social benefit. Though difficult, it is not impossible, and researchers such as Erikson and Kotre describe many examples from their interviews with older adults, particularly those who play mentor and grandparent roles.[7]

After the fisherman presents the Sultan with the four fish, the Sultan becomes the main character. I shall skip over the details of the Sultan's adventures to focus on the final outcome. A bewitched land is emancipated, its Prince freed, and its people restored to their human form. The fisherman is personally rewarded by the Sultan and the Prince, but the individuals who benefit the most are the Prince and his people. So the emancipation of society and the fisherman's good fortune occur together.

This theme is not a fantasy found only in fairy tales. In later life, many individuals consciously turn toward social causes and work for the emancipation of society.[8] Benjamin Spock provides a dramatic illustration. He was perhaps the most famous pediatrician in America, and a whole generation of parents followed his advice in raising their children. In his 80's, however, Spock joined young men and women in protesting the Vietnam War—at a time when such protests were still unpopular. He risked arrest and the prospect of losing his hard-won reputation. Emancipated innocence and the emancipation of society converged for him.

Because there was a prominent youth movement going on, we might think that Spock merely followed others and that his case reflects the turbulence of the 1960's more than personal development. But Spock's is not an isolated example. Two centuries earlier, the French satirist Voltaire followed a similar course.[9] Although fearless in his writing, he was quite cautious—even timid—in his personal life. In his late 60's, however, he abandoned prudence and became personally involved in several controversial causes. He sought to overturn what he perceived to be gross injustices, and his championship of those causes forced him to flee from France on several occasions. He gave up a secure and comfortable life to seek the emancipation of society.

An even more delightful example comes from the life of Okubo Hikozayemon, a 16th century Japanese lord.[10] Late in life, Okubo was the confidante of the Shogun, the supreme ruler of feudal Japan. As a reward for Okubo's invaluable services, the Shogun offered to make Okubo a great lord with corresponding honor and authority. Okubo declined the offer. He asked, instead, to have a special favor conferred upon him—to be granted immunity from any legal punishment, no matter what he did. The request was unprecedented, but then so was the Shogun's gratitude. The Shogun agreed. Okubo then went around the country chastising the lords and princes of the realm whenever they did something wrong. Okubo played the part of the gadfly, like the aged Socrates, mocking people in order to right wrongs. Okubo would have been seized and executed at once by the proud lords, just as Socrates was, except, of course, that Okubo had been granted legal immunity beforehand. Legend has it that Okubo even made fun of the Shogun himself. The Shogun had a cherry tree that he prized dearly, ordering that anyone who harmed the tree be executed. So Okubo went to the tree and tore off a branch, protesting the cruel and absurd law. The Shogun recognized his error and rescinded his decree.

There is one final and very important point in the story of "The Fisherman and the Djinn." It is the story of elder tales themselves, and how they were lost and forgotten in recent times.

Bruno Bettelheim analyzed "The Fisherman and the Djinn" in his insightful book.[11] The story, Bettelheim noted, has an important message for children. The djinn symbolizes the child's anger—which children often fear they cannot control. But the fisherman's clever ruse to get the djinn back into the bottle reassures the child that he can, indeed, outsmart his own anger and control his emotions. As a psychoanalyst who worked with children, Bet-

126

telheim understandably emphasized the relevance of the story to youth, rather than adults. So he did not discuss the psychology of aging contained in the tale. Indeed, when Bettelheim summarized the fairy tale, he presented a truncated version, in which the fisherman throws the flask into the sea after tricking the djinn back into the bottle.

But the original story just starts to get interesting there. This inadvertent editing is not unusual, either. From the time fairy tales were first published, they have been simplified and edited— by publishers as well as commentators.[12] In the process, the role of older adults in fairy tales appears to have been downgraded or even eliminated. Evidence for this editing can be seen by comparing "The Fisherman and the Djinn" with other fairy tales. Notice that the present story falls into two parts. The first half focuses on the old fisherman and his adventures. Then in the second part, the tale shifts to a younger protagonist—the Sultan. The story emphasizes the difference in age between the two men by calling the fisherman "well-stricken in years," and specifying that he has three *adult* children. The Sultan, by contrast, apparently has no family yet. Moreover, the Sultan is called neither young nor old, and this is characteristic of middle-aged individuals in other fairy tales.[13] We saw the same thing in "The Widow and the Frog," where the first half emphasizes the widow, and the second, the young man, alias the frog. The important thing about these two stories is that they give *equal time* to the older and younger protagonists, and the structure is typical of elder tales in general.

Indeed, if we look carefully at most fairy tales, we discover the same two-part structure. But the majority of youth tales severely abbreviate the first half of the story. So the struggles and concerns of the older protagonist are given short shrift. The Grimms' story about Thumbling provides an illustration. In the tale, an old couple bewail their lack of children. The old woman declares she would be happy even if she had a son no bigger than her thumb and she soon gives birth to just such a child. After offering the old couple a dozen lines, the story shifts to a long chronicle about Thumbling's exploits. His parents' story receives little attention, and their personal conflicts are barely mentioned. Other examples are easy to find.[14] Taken together, they suggest that most familiar fairy tales are simplified or fragmented versions of stories in which

127

elders played a larger role. To be sure, the reasoning here is inferential, and may seem a bit tenuous, but it is similar to the deductions that paleontologists make, reconstructing dinosaurs from fossil fragments. Moreover the hypothesis that fairy tales are derived from more complete sagas is not new: the brothers Grimm themselves postulated that the fairy tales they collected were remnants of older, more complex myths.[15] Fortunately, enough elder tales have survived to this day that we can rescue them from obscurity. And more importantly, as folklore scholars have noted, fairy tales are sturdy enough to have retained their insights about human nature.[16] Even when the plots and characters have been altered, elder tales still offer invaluable counsel for the second half of life.

15

The Old Man Who Made Withered Trees Flower

(from Japan)

Once upon a time, a kind old man and his wife lived alone with a little white dog. They had everything they needed, except for children, and so they lavished their affections on their pet.

One day, the dog kept barking in the yard, and the old man went out to see what was the matter. The dog ran repeatedly to a spot just beneath a large tree, and the old man figured his pet had found something buried there. So he fetched his spade, and dug. To his surprise, he unearthed a cache of gold coins! He called his wife outside, and the two hugged their little white dog.

Now the kind old man and his wife had a neighbor who was a wicked, greedy man. This neighbor often threw stones at the little white dog, or kicked him whenever no one was looking. The wicked neighbor had heard the dog barking, and so he watched the old man dig up the treasure. The next day, the wicked neighbor asked the kind old man if he could borrow the dog for the day. The kind man thought this was peculiar since his neighbor had never like animals, but the old man was too generous to refuse.

The wicked man then took the little white dog to his own yard. "If you found a treasure for your master, you can find me one, too!" and the greedy man forced the poor animal to sniff the ground. The dog stopped beneath a large tree, and the villain immediately started digging. He labored for many hours and then uncovered a pile of filthy refuse. The wicked man became soiled and this enraged him so much, he struck the little dog with his spade and killed him. Then he buried the animal in the hole.

A few days later, the kind old man came calling and asked for his dog back. "I had to kill your vicious dog in self-defense!" the wicked neighbor said, "and I buried the wretched creature under a tree."

The kind old man was heartbroken. He knew his dog would never attack anybody, but he said nothing. He only asked his neighbor for the tree under which his pet was buried. "I will make a memorial to him," the old man explained. The wicked neighbor could not very well refuse and so the old man took the tree home.

The old man then carved a mortar and pestle out of the wood. "This way," he explained to his wife, "we can make rice cakes in memory of our dog." They both recalled how much their pet had liked the pastries. So the old man and his wife put rice in the mortar to pound into sweet dough. But before they did anything, cakes came pouring out from the mortar. "It is the spirit of our dear dog!" they exclaimed. And when they tasted the rice cakes, they were more delicious than any they had eaten before.

All this the wicked neighbor saw and so he came over to borrow the magic mortar. The old man was reluctant to lend it to him, but he was too kind to refuse. So the wicked neighbor took the magic mortar home. But when he tried to pound rice in it, only foul wastes came pouring out. In a rage, he burned the mortar. A few days later, the kind old man requested the return of his mortar, and the wicked man said he burned it. "Ah," the old man lamented. "It was a memento of my little dog." He thought a moment, and then asked for the ashes of the mortar. "They can be a memorial, too." The evil neighbor could not refuse, and the old man returned home and saved the ashes in a basket.

One day, the wind blew some of the ashes into the cherry trees in the old man's yard. It was winter, and the trees were bare of leaves. But the moment the ashes hit the branches, they burst into blossom, as if it were spring. Word spread quickly and soon people from all the land came to admire the cherry trees. One day, a samurai came calling, and told the old man that the Lord of the land wanted to see him. The samurai explained that the Lord's favorite cherry tree had withered and died, and the Lord wondered if the old man could make the tree blossom again. The kind old man said he would try, and fetched his magic ashes.

The samurai took the old man to the palace, and there before all the nobles and warriors, the old man climbed into the dead tree. He lifted his basket of ashes and threw the dust into the barren boughs. The tree immediately burst into bloom, filling the palace with bright colors and sweet scents. The Lord was deeply grateful, and bestowed upon the old man great riches and the title, "He Who Makes Withered Trees Blossom."

All this the wicked neighbor heard about. So he gathered ashes from his fireplace, and the next day he went walking through town saying, "I am the man who makes withered trees blossom." The Lord heard him, and called him in.

"But you are not the same man I talked to yesterday!" the Lord exclaimed.

"No," the wicked neighbor said, "I am his teacher." So the Lord asked the wicked man to make another withered tree bloom. The greedy neighbor eagerly climbed into the tree, and threw ashes on the branches. But nothing happened. He threw more ashes, until they flew all over the Lord and the assembled nobles. Still the bare tree did not blossom. So the Lord cast the wicked man into prison for being an impostor.

As for the kind old man and his wife, they lived in happiness and honor until the day they died. And every day, even in the depth of winter, their home was surrounded by fragrant blossoms.

Summarized from "The Old Man Who Made Withered Trees Flower," in Y. T. Ozaki, The Japanese Fairy Book (Tokyo: Tuttle, 1970) and F. H. Mayer, Ancient Tales in Modern Japan (Bloomington, Ind.: Indiana University Press, 1985).

Reflections: Return and Transfiguration

This charming story elaborates on one last development which we have touched upon in various elder tales. It is the theme of reclaiming the magic and wonder of childhood, returning at the end of life to the beginning, but to one transfigured and illuminated.

Our story presents the theme of return and transfiguration in an unusually complicated sequence of magic objects. The old man and woman lavish their care on a *dog* who uncovers a cache of *gold* coins for them, but only foul refuse for their wicked neighbor. After the evil neighbor kills the dog, the old man makes a *mortar* which then magically produces *food* for him, but wastes for his neighbor, so the evil neighbor burns the mortar, leaving the kind old man *ashes*. Quite by accident one day in winter, the old man discovers that the ashes transform *withered trees* into ones full of *blossoms*.

From the outset, this sequence is striking because most elder tales do not focus so much on magical objects. As we discussed earlier, tales of youth typically dwell on *things*, while elder tales emphasize psychological *insights*. So we might suspect that the sequence has special symbolic meaning.

Each of these objects captures an important and fearful stereotype of aging. First consider the dog. The story tells us that the old couple dearly wanted children, but never had any. So they lavish their affection upon the dog, as if he were their child. This conjures up a poignant stereotype of old age—the lonely old man or woman who has outlived friends and family, and who must now turn to a pet for comfort. Indeed, of all the deprivations of old age, loneliness and bereavement are surely among the heaviest.

In the tale, the dog is energetic and cheerful, bringing new life to the old man and his wife. The dog thus contrasts with the gold that appears next in the story. Cold and lifeless, the gold was hoarded by someone long ago, and points to another common stereotype of aging—the miser, who cares only for money and spurns the warmth of human relationships, valuing possessions rather than wisdom. The story highlights the miser theme by introducing the greedy neighbor next door who wants a treasure for himself, and who kills the little dog when thwarted. The wicked neighbor values gold more than life itself.

The story then introduces a mortar which magically produces food. This hints at another fearful outcome of old age—the elderly person no longer concerned with anything but eating. This is often painfully evident in nursing homes, where individuals may not have family or friends to visit. Lacking the opportunity for human company, or the ability to pursue rewarding activities, the frail old person often can look forward only to meals. The ashes that appear next in the story have an equally sad symbolism—they point to decline and death, as do the withered trees and the winter setting of the tale.

By presenting its succession of symbolic objects, our story depicts a specter most adults fear in old age: progressive deterioration until one becomes a helpless infant again, having to be cleaned and fed. Such a fear of regression with old age lies deep in folklore. Many cultures speak with disgust about "second childhood." And poets from time immemorial have made frequent—usually horrified—comparisons between decrepit old adults and helpless children.[1] This regression occurs in cases of a disease like Alzheimer's,[2] where the ability to relate to other people deteriorates until the individual often relates only to pets or dolls. With further decline, the individual may hoard things like food, and finally become unable even to feed him- or herself.

Although only a small number of individuals deteriorate in this dramatic fashion, psychologists have documented subtler decrements that accompany aging. As mentioned before, standardized test scores on memory, perception, and abstract reasoning tend to decline with age, and these changes were initially interpreted as signs of *intellectual* regression in old age—the loss of higher mental functioning.[3] Psychoanalysts in their turn have commented on *emotional* regression in later life, and particularly how older individuals often return to earlier, immature emotional levels.[4] Psychoanalytic theories of development are particularly relevant here, because they provide another interpretation for the unique succession of objects in our story.

Readers may be familiar with Freud's view that children develop through distinct stages, beginning with the oral stage, proceeding to the anal, and thence to the phallic and genital stages. The oral stage is that of infancy, where the infant puts everything in his mouth, edible or not. The anal stage characterizes the toddler, and especially the period of toilet training, where anal control is the focus. The phallic stage comes later, when little boys like to show off their phalluses, and see those of other people. Children at this stage are preoccupied with issues of power and aggression. Finally, the genital stage is that of mature adulthood, involving procreative sexuality.[5] Psychoanalysts from various schools have commented on how old age reverses the sequence, so that the older individual moves backward from the mature genital stage, to the phallic, anal, and thence to the oral. More systematic research tends to confirm this observation.[6] Older persons make more oral references in response to the Rorshach Inkblot Test, for instance. The present story symbolizes this psychological regression in its unusual sequence of objects.

The story begins by noting that the old couple are childless and so focus their affection on their dog. Since children are the product of genital sexuality, the fact that the old man and woman do not have any offspring suggests they have regressed from the genital stage of development. The little dog in fact makes a passable symbol of the phallic stage, since the dog is a powerful, aggressive creature, and those are features of the phallic stage. Gold is introduced next, and is usually interpreted in psychoanalytic terms as a symbol for the anal stage. Misers in general, according to psychoanalytic theory, are preoccupied with issues from the anal stage of development, and particularly with hoarding things. The story confirms the anal theme in a hilarious way when the wicked old man goes looking for a treasure and digs up foul wastes, suggestive of excrement. The mortar that comes next produces food and offers a transparent symbol of oral gratification. So the objects in the tale can be interpreted in one stroke by the traditional psychoanalytic view of development—they depict a process of psychological regression from the genital, back to the phallic, anal, and oral stages.

The tale does not stop with the theme of regression, however, but turns the motif on its head. After losing his dog, and the magic mortar, the old man is left with ashes, but the ashes make withered trees blossom. Far from ending in dissolution, then, the story leads to renewal and rejuvenation: spring appears in the middle of winter. In making withered trees blossom, the magic ashes recall a theme we discussed earlier—inanimate things come to life, and magic awakens in the world. So the miraculous ashes can be interpreted as a symbol for the return of wonder in later life. The story does not depict mere regression, then, but rather the reclamation of long-lost virtues—innocence, spontaneity, and delight.

As mentioned before, more careful research in the psychology of aging suggests that what seems on first appearances to be regression in old age is actually conscious choice.[7] If older adults cite idiosyncratic personal experiences in solving problems, rather than abstract rules of logic the way young adults do, it is often because the mature adult deliberately uses simpler modes of reasoning to fit a problem at hand. As one older individual said, in explaining her reasoning on a problem, "Why use a computer to add $2 + 2$?" "By now I know I can trust my intuition," said another, explaining how he often decided against a logical, step-by-step analysis of problems. What appears to be regression is actually a conscious affirmation of a more mythic, intuitive variety of reasoning.[8]

The return to earlier modes of consciousness frequently takes the form of reminiscing in later life. As the French novelist Charles Nodier observed, "The kindest privilege that Nature grants the aging man is that of reclaiming the impressions of his childhood with extraordinary ease."[9] And modern studies confirm the observation: reminiscence becomes increasingly important to individuals as they age.[10] In remembering the past, though, older adults transform it. The reflective individual comes to terms with mistakes and opportunities missed, ideally learning to forgive himself—and others. Events and actions that once seemed inexplicable make sense in retrospect. The return to the past in memories transfigures the effect of the past on the present.

In many ways, though, personal recollections offer only a diminished form of reminiscence. In traditional cultures, older adults recounted the legends, myths—and fairy tales—of their people. The narration allowed the elders to return psychologically to "the beginning time," before the creation of the world or the appearance of man—not just to a personal past, but to a collective one. This is a deeper and more moving reminiscence,[11] which is difficult to experience in contemporary secular society. Such a collective remembrance is not impossible, however, even now, because mythology, history, philosophy, literature, and art remain. Each offers a chance to experience a collective form of return and transfiguration.

The process can also be seen in grandparents playing with their grandchildren. Indeed, the tie between the two generations is a special one, seen in many cultures. Grandparent and grandchild joke, tease, and play with one another, relatively free from the inhibitions or reservations that parents must observe.[12] If the elders pass on vital knowledge to their grandchildren, the grandchildren return the favor by offering their elders the magic of childhood. Dr. C, a professional colleague of mine, dramatized the point in his 60's. A distinguished academic scientist by profession, white-haired and dignified, Dr. C changed profoundly with the birth of his first grandchild. When he played with his granddaughter, he crawled gleefully on all fours and romped with the family cat and dog. He read stories to his granddaughter, and laughed as much as she did. Through his time with her, he gradually reclaimed the spontaneity and delight he had forgotten over the years of his professional life. The transformation was soon noticeable to his staff. Previously stern and formal, Dr. C began playing small, good-natured practical jokes on his staff, and they on him. The rigid, cerebral tone of his research laboratory lightened up considerably.

The story of "The Old Man Who Made Withered Trees Flower" reveals a paradox. The mature adult moves backwards, later in life, returning to the earliest stage of psychological development. But that stage then becomes something "higher." The elder embraces the past, not to regress, but to illuminate all of life. The end is the beginning, transfigured.

16
The Shining Fish
(from Italy)

nce upon a time, an old man and his wife lived in a house overlooking the sea. Through the years, all their sons died, leaving the old couple to poverty and loneliness. The old man barely earned a living by gathering wood in the forest and selling it in the village. One day in the wilderness, he met a man with a long beard. "I know all about your troubles," the stranger said, "and I want to help." He gave the old man a small leather bag and when the old man looked in it, he fainted with surprise: the bag was filled with gold! By the time the old man came to, the stranger was gone. So the old man threw away his wood, and rushed home. But along the way, he began to think. "If I tell my wife about this money, she will waste it all," he told himself. And so when he arrived at home, he said nothing to his wife. Instead, he hid the money under a pile of manure.

The next day, the old man awoke to find that his wife had cooked a wonderful breakfast, with sausages and bread. "Where did you find the money for this?" he asked his wife.

"You did not bring any wood to sell yesterday," she said, "so I sold the manure to the farmer down the road." The old man ran out, shrieking with dismay. Then he glumly went to work in the forest, muttering to himself.

Deep in the woods, he met the stranger again. The man with the long beard laughed. "I know what you did with the money, but I still want to help." So he gave the old man another purse filled with gold. The old man rushed home, but along the way he started thinking again. "If I tell my wife, she will squander this fortune. . . . " And so he hid the money under the ashes in the fireplace. The next day he awoke to find his wife had cooked another hearty breakfast. "You did not bring back any firewood," she explained, "so I sold the ashes to the farmer up the road."

The old man ran into the forest, pulling out his hair in consternation. Deep in the wilderness, he met the stranger a third time. The man with the long beard smiled sadly. "It seems you are not destined to be rich, my friend," the stranger said. "But I still want to help." He offered the old man a large bag. "Take these two dozen frogs, and sell them in the village. Then use the money to buy the largest fish you can find—not dried fish, shellfish, sausages, cakes, or bread. Just the largest fish!" With that the stranger vanished.

The old man hurried to the village and sold his frogs. Once he had the money in hand, he saw the wonderful things he could buy at the market, and he thought the stranger's advice odd. But the old man decided to follow the instructions, and bought the largest fish he could find. He returned home too late in the evening to clean the fish, so he hung it outside from the rafters. Then he and his wife went to bed.

That night, it stormed, and the old man and woman could hear the waves thundering on the rocks below their house. In the middle of the night, someone pounded on the door. The old man went to see who it might be, and found a group of young fishermen dancing and singing outside.

"Thank you for saving our lives!" they told the old man.

"What do you mean?" he asked. So the fishermen explained that they were caught at sea by the storm, and did not know which way to row until the old man put out a light for them. "A light?" he asked. So they pointed. And the old man saw his fish hanging from the rafters, shining with such a great light it could be seen for miles around.

From that day on, the old man hung out the shining fish each evening to guide the young fishermen home, and they shared their catch with him. And so he and his wife lived in comfort and honor the rest of their days.

Summarized from "Shining Fish" in I. Calvino, Italian Folk Tales *(New York: Pantheon, 1978).*

Reflections: The Elder Cycle Completed

The story of "The Shining Fish" brings this anthology to an end and the tale is doubly qualified to serve as the conclusion. The story contains all the themes we have discussed till now and portrays the complete drama of elder tales. That drama, in turn, symbolizes the psychological tasks adults must master in maturity. In essence, this final tale depicts an ideal journey through the second half of life. Moreover, the story is one of the few elder tales from Europe, having survived the editing which makes these stories rare in Western folklore. That alone makes it significant.

The story opens with an old man and his wife living in poverty—a theme present in virtually every elder tale. To make this specter of loss even more dramatic, the story says that the old couple's children all died. So they have sustained perhaps the deepest grief an adult can suffer.[1] By beginning with such a dismal picture, this story warns us—like other elder tales—that it will not gloss over the problems of growing old. It then proceeds to show how the individual can deal with the losses of aging.

The old couple lives on the seashore at the edge of a forest. So they occupy the boundary between land and sea, on one hand, and wilderness and civilization on the other hand. We saw the same setting in "Fortune and the Woodcutter," "The Simple Grasscutter," and "The Fisherman and the Djinn." The marginal location symbolizes the boundary between conscious and unconscious, and reflects a central theme in elder tales: confronting neglected aspects of the self, hidden in the unconscious. The present story underscores the theme by saying that the old man gathers wood from the forest for a living. As we saw, wood-gathering—and fishing, for that matter—appears in elder tales from around the world, and symbolizes the process of recovering material from the unconscious.

The old man then meets a stranger who gives him a bag of gold. This is the next theme of elder tales: magic returns unexpectedly, and in the course of ordinary events. Like the old man in "Fortune and the Woodcutter," or the old woman in "The Widow and the Frog," the present protagonist does not seek fortune in far-off lands. The stranger comes to him unbidden, and the old man's task is to *notice and accept* the magic. After all, if the old man were suspicious or hostile and fled the stranger, nothing would have happened. He would not have developed further.

After receiving the gold from the stranger, the old man hides it without telling his wife. He acts out of suspicion and greed, and the fact that the old man conceals the gold under *manure* emphasizes the odious nature of his motivations. When the old man's wife inadvertently sells the manure the next day, the old man is punished for his avarice. While this is the usual outcome for wicked people in fairy tales about youth, the present tale goes on. The old man receives another bag of gold from the stranger, and hides it again, still acting out of suspicion and greed, but a little less so than previously: the ashes in which he hides the gold are not as foul as manure. The old man loses his money anyway. Repeated misfortunes like this are common in tales of youth. There, though, the youth typically fails because he confronts a powerful adversary like a wicked witch, or an evil ring. Here the old man has a magic ally in the stranger. Indeed, the old man's enemy is his *own* greed and suspicion. Losing the gold thus forces him to face his own shadow side, and this is the next theme of elder tales: self-confrontation and self-reformation. If he continued to pursue his own greedy notions, the old man would not have bought the fish, as the stranger suggested, and again no further development would have occurred.

The present story also portrays the theme of deception and wisdom at this point. The old man hides his gold in manure and ashes, thinking reasonably enough that nobody would look for a treasure in them. In elder tales like "The Old Alchemist," this kind of deception constitutes wisdom—the psychologically astute use of illusions. Here the old man's trick backfires, and we might speculate that it does so because the old man acts out of greed. He has not mastered his own Shadow, and such self-mastery is a prerequisite of true wisdom, as dramatized in "The Wise Merchant" and "The Old Alchemist." Cunning is not wisdom, elder tales say— cunning with care is.

When the stranger appears a third time, he offers the old man both a bag of frogs and some advice. I will return to the symbolism of the frogs shortly, after focusing on the stranger's advice. Those comments seem odd, as the old man realizes when he thinks about what else he could buy with his money. But the old man obeys the stranger, and purchases the largest fish he can find. We might infer that the old man heeds the advice because he knows by now how poor his own judgment can be: he has lost a fortune twice. In essence, the old man finally transcends his own greed and egocentricity. This self-transcendence is the next theme of elder tales.

The stranger's identity becomes easier to interpret now. A magical being, apparently knowledgeable about everything that happens, the stranger makes a good symbol for something that transcends the conscious, rational self. From a Jungian perspective, the stranger symbolizes the inner Self—an image of psychological completion and integration, like the Dragon King in the story of that name. From a religious viewpoint, the stranger could be a representative of God, possessing transcendent knowledge, like the aunt in "An Old Mother's Sorrow." In any case, he appears to be something higher than normal ego consciousness.

After buying the largest fish he can find, the old man returns home and hangs it outside from the rafters. Doing so seems odd, even in an age without refrigerators. Since the fish dangles in the open, the old man runs the risk of having it stolen, whether by man, cat, or bird! So the old man trusts that he will not lose his gift and his faith is at once innocent and foolish. This paradoxical attitude brings up the theme of emancipated innocence. Having confronted his greed, mastered it, and transcended himself, the old man can now trust the intuitions of his heart. He no longer

143

tries to hoard the stranger's gifts for himself, and instead symbolically offers the fish to the world.

That night, a terrible storm breaks out and threatens the lives of several young fishermen. They are saved by the old man's shining fish. The story thus portrays the final development in elder tales: the old man brings magic into the world which helps the next generation. He mediates between this realm and the next, benefitting society. This is, of course, the typical role of the elder in fairy tales of youth—the good witch or the helpful fairy godmother who rescues a young man or woman from some dreadful danger. "The Shining Fish" is important in showing how the elder gains the "magic" and wisdom—through a long process of psychological development.

Notice how the old man's mediating role shifts. Initially, he mediates between himself and the stranger, for his own personal benefit, keeping the gold for himself. Here the stranger can be taken as a symbol of the old man's unconscious, so that the relationship between the two involves introspection. Talking to the stranger symbolizes a process of self-exploration. As discussed before, such introversion is important in the second half of life, when personal reminiscence, and philosophical reflection increase, but the story adds further insight. When the old man hangs the shining fish out each night, he mediates between supernatural powers on one hand, and youth on the other. This new role is social, not solitary—oriented toward other people, not the inner self. Ultimately, the next generation benefits. The story thus emphasizes that the emancipation of society, and not just the self, is the final goal in the second half of life.

As the drama of "The Shining Fish" unfolds, it also depicts a return to progressively earlier developmental levels, so that the end is the beginning, transfigured. This is an underlying theme in elder tales, conveyed by a succession of symbolic objects in the present story. The narrative begins with *gold*, moves on to *frogs*, and ends up with a *fish* that is soon transformed into a shining *light*. Here a mythological framework for interpretation is useful because gold, frogs, and fish appear frequently in myths and legends around the world. Gold, for example, is typically a symbol of human culture and human consciousness.[2] The color of the sun is gold, and the sun—indeed, light in general—symbolizes consciousness. Gold is also used for money in virtually every society. So gold symbolizes secular life and civilization: the highest measure of man's consciousness.

The story quickly dispenses with the gold, not once but twice, in case we missed the importance of the event. Material reward and secular achievement are not the goals of the second half of life. Frogs appear next in the story, and their symbolism is complex and profound. Since frogs are amphibious animals that inhabit the boundary between water and land, they make excellent symbols of the transition from unconscious to conscious. We saw this in "The Widow and the Frog," and frogs play the same role in the present tale, except in the reverse direction. The old man goes from the conscious to unconscious. First he loses gold, symbolizing culture and consciousness, and ends up with frogs instead, representing a transitional state. He then exchanges the frogs for a fish. As creatures of water, hidden from sight, fish are frequently construed as symbols of the *unconscious* by psychoanalysts and mythologists.[3] Moreover, fish are much less developed than frogs, lacking any limbs at all, so they symbolize a primitive level of existence. Our story thus depicts a shift back to earlier and earlier stages of development, just like the tale of "The Old Man Who Made Withered Trees Flower."

Frogs have another symbolic meaning—that of renewal and transfiguration. Italian folklore associates frogs with Easter and the transfiguration of Christ,[4] probably because frogs undergo a dramatic physical change around Easter, changing from tadpole to frog. Frogs therefore make a good symbol for the transformation of the material into the spiritual, the natural into the numinous. This association, I should add, holds for other cultures, like that of Tibet.[5]

The present tale immediately confirms the theme of transfiguration by introducing the fish—a fundamental symbol of Christ. (The meaning would have been known to the Italian and presumably Catholic narrators of this tale.)[6] The fish then becomes a numinous beacon symbolizing a spiritual transformation, in analogy with the transfiguration of Christ.

The fish therefore symbolizes two things at the same time—an early, basic, or primitive kind of experience, unconscious and undeveloped, on one hand, and spiritual renewal on the other. The frogs serve as a transition to both the lowest and the highest states man can experience, the beginning and the end. This theme of return and transfiguration appears throughout elder tales in various forms. We saw, for example, the theme of reclaiming the innocence and spontaneity of childhood in "The Old Man Who Lost His Wen," "The Magic Forest," and "The Six Statues."

"The Shining Fish" thus pulls together all the themes of elder tales, and reveals the underlying drama—the journey beyond the self in the second half of life, towards the illumination of society. The themes symbolize vital tasks that confront the individual from mid-life onward, and it may be useful to recapitulate those tasks.

The first challenge is dealing with the specter of decline, and the reality of multiple losses in later life: the loss of health, friends, wealth, and power. Painful as these are, these losses clear the way for new developments—they break down old routines, and make room for unexpected developments. In the process, the individual must be willing to delve into the unconscious, grappling again with psychological issues which were intolerable in youth. Age and experience provide new strength to face old fears, and the challenge of maturity is to use those assets to grow. The danger here is withdrawing from life in despair or bitterness.

Ultimately this openness to new experience depends upon confronting the dark side of human nature, and the Shadow within oneself: anger over the indignities of aging, despair over recuperating from losses, envy for what younger people still possess, and greed for more in life. Self-confrontation and self-reformation comprise the second task, and failure in this task leads to meanness of spirit and a stunted soul.

From self-confrontation comes an understanding of evil, and that in turn gives rise to worldly wisdom: the ability to create convincing illusions, based on psychological insights, for the benefit of other people. This is a third task of later life: to turn from the youthful preoccupation with things—manipulating objects and accumulating possessions—to an empathic understanding of human nature. Such worldly wisdom helps the individual protect himself from more powerful adversaries and adapt to the stresses of later life. In a sense, wisdom is the reward for honest self-confrontation. Survival and adaptation, however, are not the ulti-

146

mate goals of life, and the individual soon confronts a new, and more difficult challenge—that of self-transcendence.

This fourth task is to break free of the personal ambitions and dreams which dominate youth. Ironically, if the focus of the first half of life is establishing the self, the challenge of maturity is leaving that hard-won self behind. Erikson's concept of generativity is one example of self-transcendence, but there are many other forms, psychological or religious. Ideally, the mature adult returns to the transcendent inspirations of his or her youth, but in a deeper way, with greater understanding, and with the means to actualize some of those dreams. These transcendent inspirations can be overwhelming in their intensity, so the strength, patience and wisdom of age are essential. Noble concerns, in all their uplifting and terrifying aspects, now take precedence over purely personal desires. The higher Self, Society, or God replaces the ego as the guiding force in life.

With the ability to transcend a purely egocentric perspective, the elder can now safely abandon social conventions, and this becomes the fifth task: to break from the pragmatic rationality that dominates the middle years and liberate oneself from social customs. Emancipated innocence—the reclamation of the child's spontaneity—is ideally the result. Yet adult rationality and social conventions are not sacrificed. Innocence and sagacity must be integrated and the child's native creativity united with mature judgment. The challenge here is heeding the natural dictates of the soul, purified through a long process of self-confrontation and self-transcendence. The individual can then affirm his or her own life, just as it is. And this is the attitude Erikson called integrity. Without such affirmation, despair and stagnation await the aging individual—hypochondriasis and a gradual descent into misery. Emancipated innocence is not merely a virtue of later life, it is a necessity.

Understood and nurtured, emancipated innocence blossoms into a renewal of the mythic mode of experience. And this is the sixth task depicted in elder tales: the reclamation of wonder and delight in life. The world is then no longer taken for granted, and each object becomes an occasion for delight. The adult returns to a mature form of animism and mythic experience, almost mystical in nature. This return of wonder resembles what many spiritual traditions call enlightenment, and though rare, it is one of the highest forms in which magic returns in the second half of life.

Yet personal illumination is not the final goal. The real challenge comes next: taking the transcendent inspirations of later life, and using them to help the next generation. This is the elder's role as mediator, linking this world with the next. The seventh and final task is to provide both practical counsel and noble inspiration for youth, helping them to balance numinous revelations with the pragmatic needs of human society.

Throughout elder tales in general, magic appears frequently, as it does in any fairy tale. But in elder tales the magic is psychological and spiritual, not merely physical and material. It is the miracle of self-reformation, self-transcendence, emancipated innocence, and the emancipation of society. The magic is a promise of renewal and a challenge to growth. On this note "The Shining Fish" ends, sounding the final chord of elder tales: the last of life becomes the first, uniting wisdom and innocence, pragmatism and magic. The end is the beginning, renewed and restored.

17

Conclusion: In the Ever After

Elder tales differ dramatically from familiar stories like "Sleeping Beauty," or "Thom Thumb." And behind the contrasting dramas lie two divergent ideals of human life—the Hero and the Elder.

The tale of the hero or heroine begins when a young man or woman leaves home to escape oppression or poverty. The youth dreams of fabulous treasure, or true love, and both can only be found in far-away lands. The symbolic meaning of the departure is understandable because adolescents must leave the psychological security of their families to "find themselves." Action is the keynote here, struggle the motif, and independence, the ultimate aim.

Like the young hero, the elder in fairy tales also struggles with poverty. Indeed, the theme is much more prominent for older protagonists. However poor a youth may be, at least the future seems infinite and full of promise. Not so with the older adult, confronting the specter of decline. And unlike the hero, the elder does not leave his or her dismal situation seeking better fortune. Instead, fortune comes to him, in the middle of ordinary, everyday chores, and the elder's task is to be open to this unexpected magic. If the virtues of youth are courage, perseverance, and confidence, those of the elder are alertness, openness, and curiosity.

Along the way the young hero or heroine typically encounters a terrible enemy—a wicked witch, a monstrous ogre, or a dragon

The youth takes up arms against this dreadful opponent. And in real life, the same thing often happens: adolescents blame their problems on their parents, defy them, and so learn independence. By contrast, the elder in fairy tales encounters no external foe: the enemy lies within. Battle to the death is not possible, nor is victory an issue—rather painful insight, honest self-knowledge, and authentic reformation. If the hero struggles to change the world, the elder seeks to transform himself.

Sometimes the elder does contend with an opponent, but the enemy is not a fabulous monster. It is someone with all-too-believable motives, like a greedy individual scheming to rob the older person. Where the hero turns to swords, the elder turns to insight. Lacking the strength of youth, the elder calls upon wisdom, and diverts his enemy's attack, rather than opposing it. The young hero or heroine is not so resourceful in fairy tales, and is almost defeated by the villain—until someone comes to the rescue. That person is usually a wise elder. To the eyes of youth, the elder's help seems magical, but that is because the hero or heroine does not appreciate the elder's long history of psychological development—the experience, reflection, and growth behind their wisdom.

The mortal threats the hero faces represent the vulnerable sense of self that youth struggles with, and the hero's battle symbolizes the effort to establish and defend the self. The challenge to the elder is different—not to the elder's sense of *self*, but to the elder's sense of self-*importance*. Self-transcendence is the elder's task, self-founding, the hero's.

When the young hero or heroine defeats the enemy, he or she wins great treasure, or true love. A new world opens to them and it is now *their* world. Victory is the theme, and personal reward the outcome. And those are, in real life, the dreams of youth. For the elder, *emancipation* is the keynote, not victory, and innocence is the consequence. Indeed, the adventures of youth typically end when the young hero wins a golden treasure. By contrast, the saga of the elder typically begins when he or she *loses* that treasure. The goal of the second half of life is not private wealth, but the illumination of mankind.

Overall, the youth's quest takes him away from home, outward into the world. His direction is forward: from obscurity into prominence, from present to future, and from abstract ideals to concrete practicalities. The elder's drama goes in the other direction: back home, into the past, and toward the deeper and more fundamental strata of human experience. Hero and elder share one thing, however: they extend the boundaries of human consciousness. The hero conquers the power of the unconscious, personified by dragons and monsters, and his triumph is a victory for reason. The hero raises consciousness to its apex. The elder deepens it, illuminating the foundations of human experience. Indeed, if youth is the flower of humanity, the elder is the root, pressed against the darkness of the human heart—and the most sublime potential of man's spirit.

In conveying these messages, youth and elder tales both use metaphor, but their aims differ. Youth is a prickly time when the individual's sense of self is delicate. Young men and women jealously guard their independence and reject explicit advice. And youth often cannot deal directly with psychological conflicts because the issues are too threatening. So fairy tales offer parables. Like the old alchemist, these stories trick youth into confronting their inner conflicts.

With the experience of many years, the elder knows how to deal with emotional conflicts directly, and is less sensitive about taking advice. But the elder faces a new challenge: breaking out of social convention and practical rationality, the bondage of planning, compromising, and "fitting in." Fairy tales help with the task. They return the elder to the world of imagination. And there, in a privileged realm, individuals can abandon rationality, remember forgotten ideals and see what *can* be, rather than what simply *is*.

Youth is a heroic time. Young men and women think in terms of battle and victory, striving and triumph. But this is not merely a personal, psychological attitude. The heroic paradigm dominates much of modern culture and reverberates deeply in society.[1] We admire astronauts, Olympic athletes, and Arctic explorers because they are all heroes: they face great danger or survive grueling ordeals for the sake of a noble victory. But there is a dark side to the golden image of the hero—a fascination with power and domination. The hero draws his sword first, and talks later.

If the hero is inherently a warrior, he is also intrinsically male:

151

the heroic paradigm places men over women. It is the young man who typically goes off on a quest in myths and fairy tales, not a young woman. Indeed, the woman's role is usually to wait at home for the hero and be the beautiful prize. In fairy tales, as well as in traditional societies, glory and power go to men, not women. Our language makes this point—"heroine" derives from "hero," as if the heroine were derivative, secondary to the hero.

Elder tales offer an alternative to this heroic paradigm.[2] These stories have a message not only for individuals, but for society as a whole. Elder tales portray a new set of virtues—wisdom, not heroism. As our stories have shown, elders affirm mediation and communication, rather than battle and conquest. Faced with the djinn, the fisherman talks and tells stories. He does not seek to destroy the monster, as the young hero typically does. The elder's role is to raise bridges, not swords.

Elder tales depict the same tasks for men and women in the second half of life: self-confrontation, self-transcendence, and the emancipation of society. Neither man nor woman is put above the other. What is important in later life is being human, not merely male or female. Again, our language reflects this point. While we distinguish between "heroes" and "heroines" on the basis of sex, there is no gender for "elder." But a new dichotomy arises—between individuals who continue to grow and develop, and those who stagnate, between the "elder" and the "elderly."

In recounting the virtues of the elder, I surely do not suggest a return to gerontocracy. For one, that would be to confuse the role of the elder with actual age. Long years do not necessarily make one wise. The elder is an archetypal image, like that of the young hero. Not all youths are heroic, nor all heroes youths. But within each individual lies the heroic potential. And in just this way, not all adults become wise and enlightened as they gain in years. But within each person awaits the figure of the elder—a promise and a challenge.

Nor is the elder better than the hero. Society needs both, and as individuals, we require a balance of the two in life. Hero and elder each capture powerful visions of human potential. By themselves, each is incomplete and one-sided, apt for particular situations in life. We need courage and heroism when fighting for lofty goals, whatever the season of life. But we require illumination and transcendence after the victory. Above all, we must have wisdom to know when to grasp, and when to let go, and that is the wisdom of the elder.

In most familiar fairy tales, the Prince and Princess battle against terrible enemies and survive overwhelming ordeals. Then they meet each other, marry, and live happily ever after. And surely true love and finding one's own kingdom represent symbolic goals for all individuals. But much more remains of life in the "ever after," and perhaps the most important: restoring innocence and wonder to a world that has forgotten them. That is the ultimate promise of elder tales, and their challenge—infusing the magic of myth and childhood into real life. The end then becomes the beginning, transfigured and illuminated, for Self, Society and God.

Notes

Chapter 1

1. Bruno Bettelheim, *The Uses of Enchantment: The Meaning and Importance of Fairy Tales* (New York: Knopf, 1976), 166–183, 194–215.
See also the works by Dieckmann, Heuscher, Jones, and Luthi in the bibliography. Of particular interest is M. Tatar's book, *The Hard Facts of the Grimms' Fairy Tales* (Princeton: Princeton University Press, 1987), which was published after this manuscript was completed.

2. Of Von Franz's books, *Individuation in Fairy Tales* (Dallas: Spring Publications, 1977) is particularly relevant here. See also the works by Hart, Heuscher, and Luthi in the bibliography.
It is important to note that psychoanalytic interpretations of fairy tales have been soundly criticized for ignoring the historical and social contexts of fairy tales. See Jack Zipes, *Don't Bet on the Prince* (New York: Methuen, 1976), 1–8. Hence social and historical factors will be included in my discussions, although the emphasis will be on psychological interpretations.

3. Dieckmann is especially clear on this point. See the case vignettes in his book, *Twice-Told Tales: The Psychological Use of Fairy Tales*, trans. B. Matthews (Wilmette, Ill.: Chiron Publications, 1986). See also the works by Campbell, Grolnick, Heuscher, Jones, Neumann, Von Franz, and Tatar in the bibliography. Tatar also observes that late middle age is a time when adults become interested in fairy tales again—*The Hard Facts of the Grimms' Fairy Tales*, xiii.

4. Simone de Beauvoir, *The Coming of Age*, trans. P. O'Brian (New York: G. P. Putnam's Sons, 1972), 221.
The shorter life expectancy and relative rarity of older persons in historical periods have parallels in 20th-century pre-industrial cultures, for instance, the !Kung tribesmen of Africa, or the Quechua Indians of the Andes. See Megan Biesele and Nancy Howell, " 'The old people give you life': Aging Among !Kung Hunter-Gatherers," in Pamela Amoss and Stevan Harrell, eds., *Other Ways of Growing Old* (Palo Alto, Calif.: Stanford University Press, 1981), 81, and Allan Holmberg, "Age in the Andes," in Robert Kleemeier, ed., *Aging and Leisure: A Research Perspective into the Meaningful Use of Time* (New York: Oxford University Press, 1961), 88.

5. Only collections written in English were reviewed. The standard indices in folklore research, such as S. Thompson, *Motif-Index of Folk Literature* (Bloomington, Ind.: Indiana University Press, 1955–8), and A. Aarne and S. Thompson, *The Types of the Folktale: A Classification and Bibliography* (Helsinki: Academia Scientarium Finnica, 1961), were singularly unhelpful in locating tales with "old" protagonists. The stories in the present volume were located by simply reading through available published collections.

6. Marie-Louise Von Franz, *Shadow and Evil in Fairy Tales* (Dallas: Spring Publications, 1974), 10–12, and *The Psychological Meaning of Redemption Motifs in Fairy Tales* (Toronto: Inner City Books, 1980), 10–14. Folklorist A. Dundes

emphasizes the oral nature of fairy tales. See his article, "Fairy Tales from a Folkloristic Perspective," in *Fairy Tales and Society: Illusion, Allusion and Paradigm*, ed. R. Bottigheimer (Philadelphia: University of Pennsylvania Press, 1986), 259 – 70. M. Tatar notes the continuum between purely oral tales and wholly literary ones. See *Hard Facts of the Grimms' Fairy Tales*, 33.

Other writers emphasize that the psychological insights in fairy tales survive the inevitable alterations the stories undergo over the years. See M. Luthi, *Fairy Tales as Art Form and Portrait of Man* (Bloomington, Ind.: Indiana University Press, 1984), 134ff, 158ff; S. S. Jones, "The Structure of Snow White," in *Fairy Tales and Society*, pp. 178, 181.

7. Bettelheim, *The Uses of Enchantment*, 117. J. R. R. Tolkien makes a similar claim, in a different way. He argues that fairy tales are presented as truths, but not of the ordinary, human world—rather that of the Faerie realm. See J. R. R. Tolkien, *Tree and Leaf* (London: Allen and Unwin, 1976), 40 – 41. Dundes also emphasizes the fantasy element in fairy tales. See his article, "Fairy Tales from a Folkloristic Perspective." In *Fairy Tales and Society*, 259 – 70.

8. Zong In-Sob, ed., *Folk Tales from Korea* (New York: Grove, 1979), 14.

9. Bettelheim emphasizes this point in *The Uses of Enchantment*, 37. See also M. Tatar, *Hard Facts of the Grimms' Fairy Tales*, xv – xvi.

10. See Bettelheim, *Uses of Enchantment*, 26, and Julius A. Heuscher, *Psychiatric Study of Myths and Fairy Tales: Their Origin, Meaning and Usefulness* (Springfield, Ill.: Charles C. Thomas, 1974), 18.

Fairy tales thus also differ from *fables*, which have animals rather than people as protagonists.

11. Robert Butler, *Why Survive?* (New York: Harper and Row, 1975).

12. Trans. P. O'Brian (New York: G. P. Putnam's Sons, 1972).

13. Quoted by Simone de Beauvoir in *The Coming of Age*, 100.

14. The same pattern can be found in pre-industrial cultures today. Among the !Kung tribesmen of Africa, for instance, folkstories present older people as powerful, significant figures, who can give or take away the life of younger men and women. See Biesele and Howell, "Aging Among !Kung Hunter-Gatherers," in Amoss and Harrell, eds., *Other Ways of Growing Old*, 77 – 8.

15. One recent example is poignant: the elders of the Kirghiz tribes in Afghanistan have traditionally been the ones who entertained and educated their communities, with recitations of ancient epics, songs, and poetry. The simple introduction of the transistor radio has undermined this social role. M. Nazif Shahrani, "Growing in Respect: Aging Among the Kirghiz of Afghanistan," in Amoss and Harrell, eds., *Other Ways of Growing Old*, 189.

The historical change in attitude toward old people is also reflected in the history of the English language—progressively more pejorative terms have been used in the last three centuries. H. C. Covey, "Historical Terminology Used to Represent Older People," *The Gerontologist* 28 (1988): 291 – 7.

16. N. L. Mergler, M. Faust, and M. D. Goldstein, "Storytelling as an Age-Dependent Skill," *International Journal of Aging and Human Development* 20 (1984 – 1985): 205 – 28.

17. Jack Zipes discusses the general process in *Fairy Tales and the Art of*

Subversion: The Classical Genre for Children and the Process of Socialization (New York: Heinemann, 1983), 47, 67; and *Breaking the Magic Spell: Radical Theories of Folk and Fairy Tales*. (Austin: University of Texas Press, 1979), 3, 8. M. Tatar discusses the particular case of the Grimms' tales, and how they were progressively altered to improve their appeal to children, and thus increase sales of the work. See *Hard Facts of the Grimms' Fairy Tales*, 19.

R. Schenda summarizes the uses of fairy tales in their historical settings. See his article, "Telling Tales—Spreading Tales: Change in the Communicative Forms of a Popular Genre," in *Fairy Tales and Society*, 81ff. K. Rowe notes how the feminine dimension was edited out over the years in her article, "To Spin a Yarn: The Female Voice in Folklore and Fairy Tale," in *Fairy Tales and Society*, 62.

18. A. Dundes, "Fairy Tales from a Folkloristic Perspective," in *Fairy Tales and Society*, 259, 261; A. Tavis, "Fairy Tales from a Semiotic Perspective," in *Fairy Tales and Society*, 198.

19. Jack Zipes, *Don't Bet on the Prince*, 27; *Breaking the Magic Spell*, 21, 160ff; A. Dundes, "Fairy Tales from a Folkloristic Perspective," in *Fairy Tales and Society*, 262; R. Schenda, "Telling Tales—Spreading Tales: Change in the Communicative Forms of a Popular Genre," in *Fairy Tales and Society*, 79. Grolnick addresses some of these criticisms directed at psychoanalytic interpretations of fairy tales. See his article, "Fairy Tales and Psychotherapy," in *Fairy Tales and Society*, 205, 208.

To avoid over-interpreting idiosyncratic details, I will focus on basic *themes* in stories, and particularly on those found in *different* elder tales. The unit of analysis is not so much a particular story and its many versions, as the motifs common to different elder tales, especially from diverse cultures. However, idiosyncratic details of particular stories often add poignant or dramatic emphasis to a common theme. In those cases, I will focus on the details, but mainly to elaborate on the basic theme. This approach combines features of Propp's structural analyses with psychodynamic interpretations and is similar to that of M. Tatar. See *Hard Facts of the Grimms' Fairy Tales*, xv – xx.

Chapter 2

1. Pre-industrial societies today give the most vivid examples of this point. See Megan Biesele and Nancy Howell, " 'The old people give you life': Aging Among !Kung Hunter-Gatherers," in Pamela Amoss and Stevan Harrell, eds., *Other Ways of Growing Old* (Palo Alto, Calif.: Stanford University Press, 1981), 82, and Charles C. Hughes, "The Concept and Use of Time in the Middle-Years: The St. Lawrence Island Eskimos," in Robert Kleemeir, ed., *Aging and Leisure: A Research Perspective into the Meaningful Use of Time* (New York: Oxford University Press, 1961), 93.

2. See particularly, E. F. Raymond and T. J. Michals, "Prevalence and Correlates of Depression in Elderly Persons," *Psychological Reports* 47 (1980): 1055 – 61; and B. Gurland and P. Cross, "Epidemiology of Psychopathology in Old Age: Some Implications for Clinical Services," *Psychiatric Clinics of North America* 5 (1982): 11 – 26.

These surveys show higher rates of depressive symptoms than that found in the National Institute of Mental Health Epidemiological Catchment Area study. See J. K. Myers, M. M. Weissman, G. L. Tischler, C. E. Holzer, III, P. J. Leaf, and H. Orvaschel, "Six-month Community Prevalence of Psychiatric Disorders in Three Communities 1980–1982," *Archives of General Psychiatry* 41 (Oct 1984): 959–67.

However, the epidemiological study did not look at symptoms, but at diagnoses of depressive disorders, as defined by formal criteria. Moreover, some have argued that these criteria are constructed from data based on younger adults, and so may miss the forms that depression takes in the later years. See, for example, D. Blazer, *Depression in Later Life* (St. Louis: Mosby, 1982), 19–22; T. Brink, "Geriatric Depression and Hypochondriasis: Incidence, Interaction, Assessment and Treatment," *Psychotherapy: Theory, Research and Practice* 19 (1982): 506–11; and G. Klerman, "Problems in the Definition and Diagnosis of Depression in the Elderly," in L. D. Breslau, M. R. Haug, eds., *Depression and Aging: Causes, Care and Consequences* (New York: Springer, 1983), 7. See also Kielholz, Gerner and Blazer in the bibliography.

3. See, for example, T. McAllister, "Overview: Pseudodementia," *American of the Journal of Psychiatry* 140 (1983): 528–33, and F. Carp, "Senility or Garden-variety Maladjustment?" *Journal of Gerontology* 24 (1969): 203–8.

4. John McLeish, *The Ulyssean Adult: Creativity in the Middle and Later Years* (New York: McGraw-Hill Ryerson, 1976). See also the works by Gerald O'Collins and Hugo Munsterberg in the bibliography.

Chapter 3

1. C. G. Jung, "The Stages of Life" (1931), in *Collected Works*, vol. 8 (Princeton: Princeton University Press, 1960), para. 775. Jung's comments are scattered throughout his voluminous writing. More accessible, integrated accounts can be found in secondary sources, e.g., Edward Whitmont, *The Symbolic Quest* (Princeton: Princeton University Press, 1969), 160–9, and Robert Johnson, *He: Understanding Masculine Psychology* (New York: Perennial Library, 1976), 66.

2. C. G. Jung, "The Personal and Collective Unconscious" (1943), in *Collected Works*, vol. 7 (Princeton: Princeton University Press, 1953), para. 103n.

3. See for example, R. Anshin, "Creativity, Mid-life Crisis and Herman Hesse," *Journal of the American Academy of Psychoanalysis* 4 (1976): 215–26; L. Davidson, "Mid-life Crisis in Thomas Mann's *Death in Venice*," *Journal of the American Academy of Psychoanalysis* 4 (1976): 203–14; and P. Newton, "Samuel Johnson's Breakdown and Recovery in Middle-age: A Life-span Developmental Approach to Mental Illness and its Cure," *International Review of Psychoanalysis* 11 (1984):93–117.

Gould cites particularly poignant examples from everyday married life—R. Gould, *Transformations: Growth and Change in Adult Life* (New York: Simon and Schuster, 1978), 294–307.

4. H. Segal, "Joseph Conrad and the Mid-Life Crisis," *International Review of Psychoanalysis* 11 (1984): 3–9.

5. P. Blos, *On Adolescence: A Psychoanalytic Interpretation* (New York: Free Press, 1966), 60, 97, 183. See also C. G. Jung, "Marriage as a Psychological

Relationship" (1925), in *Collected Works*, vol. 17 (Princeton: Princeton University Press, 1954), para. 337.

6. George Vaillant, *Adaptation to Life: How the Best and the Brightest Came of Age* (Boston: Little, Brown, 1977).

7. Dorothy Eichorn, John Clausen, Norma Haan, Marjorie Honzik, and Paul Mussen, eds., *Present and Past in Middle Life* (New York: Academic Press, 1981). See in particular the following chapters: J. B. Brooks, "Social Maturity in Middle Age and its Developmental Antecedents," 244 – 69; N. Haan, "Common Dimensions of Personality: Early Adolescence to Middle Life," 117 – 54; and P. Mussen and N. Haan, "A Longitudinal Study of Patterns of Personality and Political Ideologies," 393 – 414.

8. Similar cases are described by Vaillant in *Adaptation to Life*, 187, 191.

9. Vaillant, *Adaptation to Life*, 108, 128.

10. See, for example, the studies by Baker and Wheelwright, Grotjahn (1951, 1955), Gutmann (1981), King, and Zinberg in the bibliography.

Chapter 4

1. C. G. Jung, "Psychological Types" (1921), in *Collected Works*, vol. 6 (Princeton: Princeton University Press, 1971) para. 800 – 2.

2. Hugo Munsterberg, *The Crown of Life: Artistic Creativity in Old Age* (New York: Harcourt Brace Jovanovich, 1983) 20 – 2, 27 – 9, 34 – 5.

3. The psychoanalyst Otto Kernberg has elaborated upon this phenomenon most extensively. See, for example, *Object Relations Theory and Clinical Psychoanalysis* (New York: Jason Aronson, 1976).

4. See Peter Blos, *On Adolescence: A Psychoanalytic Interpretation* (New York: Free Press, 1966), 101, 122; D. O. Offer and J. B. Offer, *From Teenage to Young Manhood: A Psychological Study* (New York: Basic Books, 1976), 62, 79.

5. See especially P. M. King, K. S. Kitchener, M. L. Davison, C. A. Parker, and P. K. Wood, "The Justification of Beliefs in Young Adults: A Longitudinal Study," *Human Development* 26 (1983): 106 – 16, and the works by Clayton, Labouvie-Vief, Perry, Riegel, and Sinnott in the bibliography.

6. See especially D. Levinson, C. N. Darrow, E. B. Klein, M. H. Levinson, and B. McKee, *The Seasons of a Man's Life* (New York: Ballantine, 1978), 245 – 51.

7. See, for instance, W. Tseng and J. Hsu, "The Chinese Attitude Toward Parental Authority as Expressed in Chinese Children's Stories," *Archives of General Psychiatry* 26 (1972): 28 – 34; N. I. Khan, *Twenty Jataka Tales* (New York: Inner Traditions International, 1985), 29 – 33; and Gerald Friedlander, *The Jewish Fairy Book* (New York: Frederick Stokes, 1920), 49 – 61.

8. E. Hodgetts, *From the Land of the Tsar* (London: Gilbert and Rivington, 1890), 53 – 64.

9. Nathan Ausubel, *A Treasury of Jewish Folklore: Stories, Traditions, Legends, Humor, Wisdom and Folk Songs of the Jewish People* (New York: Crown, 1948), 612 – 15.

Chapter 5

1. See especially the works by Clayton in the bibliography.

2. Gisela Labouvie-Vief provides an excellent theoretical discussion of this point in "Beyond Formal Operations: Uses and Limits of Pure Logic in Life-span Development," *Human Development* 23 (1980): 141 – 61. See also, G. Labouvie-Vief and M. Chandler, "Cognitive Development and Life-Span Developmental Theory: Idealistic versus Contextual Perspectives," in Paul Baltes, ed., *Life-span Development and Behavior, Volume 1.* (New York: Academic Press, 1978), 181 – 210.

Empirical support comes from Jan Sinnott's research, e.g., "Individuals' Strategies in Everyday Problem Solving: Noncognitive and Cognitive Parameters," a paper presented to the Annual Meeting of the Gerontological Society of America, San Francisco, 1983. Donald Schon also discusses the difference between pure and practical reason in *The Reflective Practitioner: How Professionals Think in Action* (New York: Basic Books, 1983).

3. "The Deluded Dragon," in Ruth Manning-Sanders, *The Red King and the Witch: Gypsy Folk and Fairy Tales* (New York: Roy, 1964), 10 – 15. A similar story, "Uncle Trak and the Last Dragon," can be found in A. Nicoloff, *Bulgarian Fairy Tales*, (Cleveland: Nicoloff, 1979), 99 – 102.

"The Groom's Crimes," in Moss Roberts, *Chinese Fairy Tales and Fantasies* (New York: Pantheon, 1979), 212 – 13; see also, "Buying Loyalty," 209 – 12.

"The Ungrateful Children," in R. Nisbet Bain, *Cossack Fairy Tales and Folk Tales* (New York: Stokes, 1895), 212 – 21; cf. a fable version of the same tale, with an aged animal as the protagonist—"The Old Dog," in *Cossack Fairy Tales*, 127 – 9. Similar tales include "Keep Your Property," in A. Nicoloff, *Bulgarian Fairy Tales*, 151 – 3; and "The Foolish Wolf," in A. N. Afanasev, *Russian Fairy Tales* (New York: Pantheon, 1945), 450 – 2.

4. See especially the works by Clayton in the bibliography.

5. Quoted in J. McLeish, *The Ulyssean Adult: Creativity in the Middle and Later Years* (New York: McGraw-Hill Ryerson, 1976), 126.

Chapter 6

1. Andrew Lang, *The Yellow Fairy Book* (1894; reprint, New York: Dover, 1960), 100 – 7.

2. "The Deluded Dragon," in Ruth Manning-Sanders, *The Red King and the Witch: Gypsy Folk and Fairy Tales* (New York: Roy, 1964), 10 – 15.

3. "The Ungrateful Children," in R. Nisbet Bain, *Cossack Fairy Tales and Folk Tales* (New York: Stokes, 1895), 212 – 21.

4. The same theme occurs in "The Old Dog," found in Bain's *Cossack Fairy Tales*, 127 – 9, where an old dog is put out to die by his master. But a wolf helps the dog to trick his master into taking him back. The wolf is typically an evil figure in folklore, and so its altruistic helping role is all the more dramatic.

Chapter 7

1. The tale also clearly depicts elder abuse—a problem only recently recognized, but portrayed in several elder tales.

2. Erik Erikson, *Identity and the Life Cycle* (New York: International Universities Press, 1959).

3. E. Erikson, J. M. Erikson and H. Q. Kivnick, *Vital Involvement in Old Age* (New York: Norton, 1986), 91.

A. Kornhaber and K. Woodward, *Grandparents/Grandchildren: The Vital Connection* (Garden City: Doubleday, 1981), 149 – 50.

4. D. J. Levinson, C. N. Darrow, E. B. Klein, M. H. Levinson, and B. McKee, *The Seasons of a Man's Life* (New York: Ballantine 1978), 97 – 101.

5. Else Frenkel, "Studies in Biographical Psychology." *Character and Personality* 5 (1936): 1 – 34. Jung also made a similar observation in "Marriage as a Psychological Relationship" (1925), in *Collected Works*, vol. 17 (Princeton: Princeton University Press, 1954), para. 331a – c.

6. George Vaillant, *Adaptation to Life: How the Best and the Brightest Came of Age* (Boston: Little, Brown, 1977), 80, 112 – 14, 232; and N. Haan, "Common Dimensions of Personality: Early Adolescence to Middle Life," in Dorothy Eichorn, John Clausen, Norma Haan, Marjorie Honzik, and Paul Mussen, eds., *Present and Past in Middle Life* (New York: Academic Press, 1981), 136.

Similar results have been found in other studies with other socio-economic groups. See M. Thurnher, "Continuities and Discontinuities in Value Orientations," in M. F. Lowenthal, M. Thurnher, and D. Chiriboga, eds., *Four Stages of Life* (San Francisco: Jossey Bass, 1975), 180 – 1; G. Vaillant and E. Milofsky, "Natural History of Male Psychological Health: IX. Empirical Evidence for Erikson's Model of th Life Cycle," *Psychiatry* 137 (1980): 1348 – 59; and L. Viney, "A Sociophenomenological Approach to Life-span Development Complementing Erikson's Sociodynamic Approach," *Human Development* 30 (1987): 125 – 36; D. Heath, "The Maturing Person," in R. Walsh and D. Shapiro, eds., *Beyond Health and Normality: Explorations of Exceptional Well-being* (New York: Van Nostrand Reinhold, 1983), 173.

7. A. B. Chinen, "Self-contexting and Psychotherapy with Older Adults," *Psychotherapy: Theory, Research, Practice* 240 (1986): 411 – 16.

8. This is the same theme we saw in "The Sparrow's Gift," where the old woman went freely into the forest, symbolizing the unconscious. Notice that in the present tale, the old woman also lives near the magic forest.

Chapter 8

1. Charles E. Curran, "Aging: A Theological Perspective," in C. LeFevre and P. LeFevre, eds., *Aging and the Human Spirit: A Reader in Religion and Gerontology* (Chicago: Exploration Press, 1981), 68 – 82. See also the works by Bianchi, Brewi and Brennan, and Van Kaam in the bibliography.

2. R. L. Katz, "Jewish Values and Socio-psychological Perspectives on Aging," in S. Hiltner, ed., *Toward a Theology of Aging* (New York: Human Sciences Press, 1975), 135 – 50.

3. D. Gutmann, "The Cross-cultural Perspective: Notes on a Comparative Psychology of Aging," in J. Birren and W. Schaie, eds., *Handbook of the Psychology of Aging* (New York: Van Nostrand Reinhold, 1977), 302 – 26; D. Gutmann, "Observations on Culture and Mental Health in Later Life," in J. E. Birren and R. B. Sloane, eds., *Handbook of Mental Health and Aging* (New York: Prentice-Hall, 1983), 429 – 47.

4. M. Biesele, and N. Howell, " 'The Old People Give You Life': Aging Among !Kung Hunter-Gatherers," in P. T. Amoss and S. Harrell, eds., *Other Ways of Growing Old* (Palo Alto, Calif.: Stanford University Press, 1981), 155 – 74; M. Nazif Shahrani, "Growing in Respect: Aging Among the Kirghiz of Afghanistan," in P. T. Amoss and S. Harrell, eds., *Other Ways of Growing Old*, 175 – 92.

See also de Beauvoir.

5. T. Wei-ming, "The Confucian Perception of Adulthood," in E. Erickson, ed., *Adulthood* (New York: Norton, 1978), 121.

6. S. Kakar, "Setting the Stage: The Traditional Hindu View and the Psychology of Erik H. Erikson," in S. Kakar, ed., *Identity and Adulthood* (Delhi: Oxford University Press, 1979), 2 – 33; S. Rhadakrishnan, C. A. Moore, *A Sourcebook in Indian Philosophy* (Princeton: Princeton University Press, 1957), 175 – 84.

7. K. Wilber, "The Pre/Trans Fallacy," *ReVision* 5 (1980): 51 – 71.

8. R. Johnson, *He: Understanding Masculine Psychology* (New York: Perennial Library, 1976); E. Jung and M. L. Von Franz, *The Grail Legend* (Boston: Sigo, 1986).

9. D. Levinson, C. N. Darrow, E. B. Klein, M. H. Levinson, and B. McKee, *The Seasons of a Man's Life*, (New York: Ballantine, 1978), 91 – 7. See also, R. Johnson, *He*, 49 – 54; and A. Van Kaam, *The Transcendent Self: Formative Spirituality of the Middle, Early and Later Years of Life* (Denville, N.J.: Dimension Books, 1979), 24 – 5.

10. Increased altruism and humanitarian concerns can be seen in longitudinal studies, like that of G. Vaillant in *Adaptation to Life*, (Boston: Little, Brown, 1977), 330 – 1, 345 – 6, and N. Haan in "Common Dimensions of Personality: Early Adolescence to Middle Life," in D. Eichorn, J. Clausen, N. Haan, M. Honzik, and P. Mussen, eds., *Present and Past in Middle Life*, (New York: Academic Press, 1981), 133. The same development has been noted in cross-sectional studies, like M. Thurnher, "Continuities and Discontinuities in Value Orientations," in M. F. Lowenthal, M. Thurnher, and D. Chiriboga, *Four Stages of Life* (San Francisco: Jossey Bass, 1975), 180, and R. Kuhlen, "Developmental Changes in Motivation during the Adult Years," in Bernice Neugarten, ed., *Middle Age and Aging* (Chicago: University of Chicago Press, 1968), 136.

There is a large, and somewhat controversial, literature on the increase in religious interest in later life. See, for instance, A. Vinson, "The Role of Religion in the Maturation of the Autonomous Adult," in J. A. Thorson and T. C. Cook, eds., *Spiritual Well-Being of the Elderly* (Springfield, Ill.: Charles C. Thomas, 1978), 127 – 36, and W. M. Swenson, "Attitudes Toward Death in an Aged Population," *Journal of Gerontology* 16 (1961): 49 – 52.

11. H. Koenig, J. Kvale, and C. Ferrel, "Religion and Well-being in Later Life," *The Gerontologist* 28 (1988): 18 – 28. A good summary of other research on

this topic can be found in H. Koenig, L. George, and I. Siegler, "The Use of Religion and Other Emotion-Regulating Coping Strategies Among Older Adults," *The Gerontologist* 28 (1988): 303 – 10.

12. C. Mindel and C. Vaughan, "A Multidimensional Approach to Religiosity and Disengagement," *Journal of Gerontology* 33 (1978): 103 – 8.

D. Moberg, "Religiosity in Old Age," *Gerontologist* 5 (1965), 78 – 87.

G. Young and W. Dowling, "Dimensions of Religiosity in Old Age: Accounting for Variation in Type of Participation," *Journal of Gerontology* 42 (1987): 376 – 80.

13. A. Chinen, "Adult Cognitive Development: The Case of Alfred North Whitehead," in *Beyond Formal Operations. Volume 3: Models and Methods in the Study of Adolescent and Adult Thought* (New York: Praeger, In Press).

The evolution of Whitehead's thought can be traced through the following of his works: *Organization of Thought, Educational and Scientific* (London: Williams and Norgate, 1917); *An Enquiry Concerning the Principles of Natural Knowledge* (Cambridge: Cambridge University Press, 1919); *The Concept of Nature* (Cambridge: Cambridge University Press, 1920); *Science and the Modern World* (New York: Macmillan, 1925); *Religion in the Making* (New York: Macmillan, 1926); and *Modes of Thought* (New York: Macmillan, 1938).

14. Else Frenkel, "Studies in Biographical Psychology," *Character and Personality* 5 (1936): 17.

15. J. Funk, "Beethoven: A Transpersonal Analysis," *ReVision* 5 (1982): 29 – 41.

16. Hugo Munsterberg, *The Crown of Life: Artistic Creativity in Old Age* (New York: Harcourt Brace Jovanovich, 1983), 7 – 8, 21, 24 – 5, 29, 32.

17. "The Land Where One Never Dies," in I. Calvino, *Italian Folktales*, trans. G. Martin (New York: Pantheon, 1978); "The Story of the Man Who Did Not Wish to Die," in Y. T. Ozaki, *The Japanese Fairy Book* (Tokyo: Charles Tuttle, 1970).

18. "The Castle of Life" from E. Laboulaye, *Laboulaye's Fairy Book: Fairy Tales of All Nations* (Great Neck, N.Y.: Core, 1976).

19. G. T. Reker, E. J. Peacock, and T. P. Wong, "Meaning and Purpose in Life and Well-being: A Life-span Perspective," *Journal of Gerontology* 42 (1987): 43 – 9.

N. Woods and K. Witte, "Life Satisfaction, Fear of Death and Ego Identity in Elderly Adults," *Bulletin of the Psychonomic Society* 18 (1981): 165 – 8.

D. Gutmann, "The Post-parental Years: Clinical Problems and Developmental Possibilities," in William Norman and Thomas Scaramella, eds., *Mid-life: Developmental and Clinical Issues* (New York: Brunner/Mazel, 1980), 38 – 52.

Chapter 9

1. C. G. Jung, "Symbols of the Mother and Rebirth" (1952), in *Collected Works*, vol. 5 (Princeton: Princeton University Press, 1956), para 320. See also, Marie-Louise Von Franz, *The Psychological Meaning of Redemption Motifs in*

Fairy Tales (Toronto: Inner City Books, 1980), 24, 28; and B. Bettelheim, *Uses of Enchantment* (New York: Knopf, 1976), 94.

2. R. Peck, "Psychological Developments in the Second Half of Life," in B. Neugarten, ed., *Middle Age and Aging* (Chicago: University of Chicago Press, 1968), 79–83; R. Peck and H. Berkowitz, "Personality and Adjustment in Middle Age," in B. L. Neugarten, ed., *Personality in Middle and Late Life: Empirical Studies* (New York: Atherton, 1964), 15–43.

3. Three different studies using cross-sectional or longitudinal methods independently stressed the importance of psychological flexibility after mid-life. See D. Spence and E. Lurie, "Style of Life," in M. F. Lowenthal, M. Thurnher, and D. Chiriboga, *Four Stages of Life* (San Francisco: Jossey Bass, 1975), 10; J. Stroud, "Women's Careers: Work, Family and Personality," in D. Eichorn, J. Clausen, N. Haan, M. Honzik, and P. Mussen, eds., *Present and Past in Middle Life* (New York: Academic Press, 1981), 379; and G. Vaillant, *Adaptation to Life* (Boston: Little, Brown, 1977), 220–2.

4. "The Demon with the Eight Faces," in R. Dorson, *Folk Legends of Japan* (Tokyo: Tuttle, 1962), and "The Kind Woodcutter," in I. Zheleznova, *Tales of the Amber Sea: Fairy Tales of the Peoples of Estonia, Latvia and Lithuania* (Moscow: Progress Publishers, 1974).

5. C. G. Jung, "The Stages of Life," (1931) in *Collected Works*, vol. 8 (Princeton: Princeton University Press, 1960), 773ff; "Marriage as a Psychological Relationship," (1925), in *Collected Works*, vol. 17 (Princeton: Princeton University Press, 1954), 338ff; and "The Psychology of the Unconscious" (1916), in *Collected Works*, vol. 7 (Princeton: Princeton University Press, 1953), para 114–6.

6. The role reversals may explain why more old women than men are initially described as nasty in elder tales—the women express their aggressive sides, while the men become more docile, so the women may appear overtly more villainous. Both men and women, however, face the task of self-confrontation and self-reformation.

7. Systematic studies on American populations include: B. Neugarten and D. Gutmann, "Age-sex Roles and Personality in Middle Age: A Thematic Apperception Study," *Psychological Monographs: General and Applied* 17 (1958): 2–34; D. Chiriboga and M. Thurnher, "Concept of Self," in M. F. Lowenthal, M. Thurnher, and D. Chiriboga, eds., *Four Stages of Life*, 64, 71, 74; and more recently, R. Hefner, M. Rebecca, and B. Oleshansky, "Development of Sex-role Transcendence," *Human Development* 18 (1975): 142–58. Giele notes the socio-historical context of gender crossovers in J. Z. Giele, "Woman's Work and Family Roles," in J. Z. Giele, ed., *Woman in the Middle Years: Current Knowledge and Directions for Research and Policy* (New York: John Wiley, 1982), 128.

Clinical studies include: R. Gould, *Transformations*, (New York: Simon and Schuster, 1978), 234–5, 246–51; R. Lewis and C. Roberts, "Postparental Fathers in Distress," in Kenneth Solomon and Norman Levy, eds., *Men in Transition: Theory and Therapy* (New York: Plenum, 1982), 199–204; and B. Turner and L. Troll, "Sex Differences in Psychotherapy with Older People," *Psychotherapy: Theory Research and Practice* 19 (1982): 419–28.

164

8. D. Raybeck, "A Diminished Dichotomy: Kelantan Malay and Traditional Chinese Perspectives," in J. K. Brown and V. Kerns, eds., *In Her Prime* (South Hadley, Mass.: Bergin and Garvey, 1985), 155 – 70; K. P. Sinclair, "A Study in Pride and Prejudice: Maori Women at Mid-life," in J. K. Brown and V. Kerns, eds., *In Her Prime*, 117 – 34; C. Hughes, "The Concept and Use of Time in the Middle Years: The St. Lawrence Island Eskimos," in Robert Kleemeier, ed., *Aging and Leisure*, (New York: Oxford University Press, 1961), 94; H. S. Sharp, "Old Age Among the Chipewyan," in P. T. Amoss and S. Harrell, eds., *Other Ways of Growing Old* (Palo Alto, Calif.: Stanford University Press, 1981), 101.

A particularly dramatic example can be found in the life of Mary Baker Eddy, founder of Christian Science; see J. Silberger, "Mourning and Transformation: How Mary Baker Eddy Found in Middle Age a Way of Making a New Life for Herself," *Journal of Geriatric Psychiatry 12* (1979): 9 – 26.

9. R. Gould, *Transformations*, 260 – 2, 265; F. Livson, "Paths to Psychological Health in the Middle Years: Sex Differences," in D. Eichorn, et al., *Present and Past in Middle Life*, 207 – 8, 214 – 5; Else Frenkel cites the case of Queen Victoria in "Studies in Biographical Psychology," *Character and Personality* 5 (1936): 18; C. Malatesta and L. Culver, "Thematic and Affective Content in the Lives of Adult Women: Patterns of Change and Continuity," in C. Malatesta and C. Izard, eds., *Emotion in Adult Development* (Beverly Hills, Calif.: Sage Publications, 1984), 186 – 7.

10. C. G. Jung, "The Psychology of the Child Archetype" (1951), in *Collected Works*, vol. 9i (Princeton: Princeton University Press, 1959), para. 268.

11. D. J. Levinson, C. N. Darrow, E. B. Klein, M. H. Levinson, and B. Mckee, *The Seasons of a Man's Life* (New York: Ballantine, 1978), 209 – 13.

12. C. G. Jung, "Psychological Types" (1921), in *Collected Works*, Vol. 6 (Princeton: Princeton University Press, 1971), para. 789 – 91; R. Assagioli, *Psychosynthesis: A Manual of Principles and Techniques* (New York: Hobbs, Dorman, 1965), 86 – 89.

13. C. G. Jung, "The Relations between the Ego and the Unconscious" (1928), in *Collected Works*, vol. 7 (Princeton: Princeton University Press, 1953), para 404; "General Problems of Psychotherapy" (1935), in *Collected Works*, vol. 16 (Princeton: Princeton University Press, 1954), para 110; cf. "The Psychology of the Unconscious" (1916), *Collected Works*, vol. 7 (Princeton: Princeton University Press, 1953), para 114 – 6.

14. Maitland, Van Kaam, Brown, and Vinson (see bibliography) discuss transcendence and age in traditional religious terms, while Buhler and Giele reconceptualize the process in purely psychological terms. Edinger and Henderson add their independent commentaries on how psychology has recently replaced religion as the vehicle for self-transcendence.

15. Allan Chinen, "Fairy Tales and Transpersonal Development in Later Life," *Journal of Transpersonal Psychology* 17 (1985): 99 – 122; for a general discussion, see Ken Wilber, *No Boundary: Eastern and Western Approaches to Personal Growth* (Boston: Shambhala, 1981).

Chapter 10

1. C. Malatesta, "Affective Development Over the Life-span: Involution or Growth?" *Merrill-Palmer Quarterly* 27 (1981): 149.

2. M. Luthi, *The Fairy Tale as Art Form and Portrait of Man*, trans. J. Erickson. (Bloomington, Ind.: Indiana University Press, 1984), 29.

3. M. L. von Franz, *Individuation in Fairy Tales* (Dallas: Spring Publications, 1977), 35 – 7.

4. E. B. Palmore and D. Maeda, *The Honorable Elders Revisited* (Durham: Duke University Press, 1986), 95 – 6; R. J. Smith, "Japan: The Later Years," in Robert Kleemeier, ed., *Aging and Leisure* (New York: Oxford University Press, 1961), 97.

5. K. Soddy, *Men in Middle Life* (Philadelphia: Lippincott, 1967), 10; C. Rustom, "The Later Years of Life," in Robert Kleemeier, ed., *Aging and Leisure*, 103.

6. M. Biesele and N. Howell, "The Old People Give You Life," in P. T. Amoss and S. Harrell, eds., *Other Ways of Growing Old* (Palo Alto, Calif.: Stanford University Press, 1981), 92; R. B. Lee, "Work, Sexuality and Aging Among !Kung Women," in J. K. Brown and V. Kerns, eds., *In Her Prime* (South Hadley, Mass.: Bergin and Garvey, 1985), 30 – 1.

7. M. Block, J. Davidson, and J. Grambs, *Women Over Forty: Visions and Realities* (New York: Springer, 1981), 15; D. A. Counts, "Tamparonga: 'The Big Women' of Kaliai," in J. K. Brown and V. Kerns, eds., *In Her Prime*, 51,61; S. de Beauvoir, *The Coming of Age*, trans. P. O'Brian (New York: G. P. Putnam's Sons, 1972), 488 – 9.

8. C. G. Jung, *Memories, Dreams, Reflections* (New York: Pantheon, 1961), 173 – 5.

9. A. Maslow, *Toward a Psychology of Being* (Princeton: Van Nostrand, 1962), 138.

10. C. Buhler, "The General Structure of the Human Life Cycle," in C. Buhler and F. Massarik, eds., *The Course of Human Life* (New York: Springer, 1968), 25; D. Heath, "The Maturing Person," in R. Walsh and D. Shapiro, eds., *Beyond Health and Normality: Explorations of Exceptional Well-Being* (New York: Van Nostrand Reinhold, 1983), 187 – 9; P. Newton, "Samuel Johnson's Breakdown and Recovery in Middle-age," *International Review of Psychoanalysis* 11 (1984): 114; P. Pruyser, "Aging: Downward, Upward or Forward," *Pastoral Psychology* 24 (1975): 114,116; A. Vinson, "The Role of Religion in the Maturation of the Autonomous Adult," in J. A. Thorson and T. C. Cook, eds., *Spiritual Well-Being of the Elderly* (Springfield, Ill.: Charles C. Thomas, 1978), 131.

Chapter 11

1. E. Erikson, *Identity and the Life Cycle* (New York: International Universities Press, 1959), 104. Cf. Erikson's more recent discussion, in E. Erikson, J. M. Erickson, and H. Q. Kivnick, *Vital Involvement in Old Age* (New York: Norton, 1986), 70 – 2.

2. Erikson, Erikson, and Kivnick, *Vital Involvement*, 45, 74; W. Gruen, "Adult Personality: An Empirical Study of Erikson's Theory of Ego Development,"

in B. L. Neugarten, ed., *Personality in Middle and Late Life* (New York: Atherton, 1964), 11; L. Viney, "A Sociophenomenological Approach to Life-span Development," *Human Development* 30 (1987): 125–36; N. Woods and K. Witte, "Life Satisfaction, Fear of Death, and Ego Identity, in Elderly Adults," *Bulletin of the Psychonomic Society* 18 (1981): 165–8.

    3. *Vital Involvement*, 108–12; V. Revere, and S. Tobin, "Myth and Reality: The Older Person's Relationship to His Past," *International Journal of Aging and Human Development* 12 (1980): 15–26.

Chapter 12

    1. R. N. Bain, *Cossack Fairy Tales and Folk Tales* (New York: Stokes, 1895).

    2. M. Berman, *The Re-enchantment of the World* (Ithaca, N.Y.: Cornell University Press, 1981), 83; M. Eliade, *Shamanism: Archaic Techniques of Ecstasy*, trans. W. R. Trask (1951; reprint, Princeton: Princeton University Press, 1964), 94; C. G. Jung, "After the Catastrophe" (1945), in *Collected Works*, vol. 10 (Princeton: Princeton University Press, 1964), para 431; E. Neumann, *The Origins and History of Consciousness* (Princeton: Princeton University Press, 1954), 266–7.

    3. M. Berman provides a provocative discussion of the cultural and historical dimensions of this process in *The Re-enchantment of the World*, 117.

    4. N. W. Sheehan, D. E. Papalia-Finlay, and F. H. Hooper, "The Nature of the Life Concept Across the Life-span," *International Journal of Aging and Human Development* 12 (1981): 1–13; and D. E. Papalia and D. D. Bielby, "Cognitive Functioning in Middle and Old Age Adults: A Review of Research Based on Piaget's Theory," *Human Development* 17 (1974): 424–43.

    5. D. Gutmann, "An Exploration of Ego Configurations in Middle and Later Life," in B. L. Neugarten, ed., *Personality in Middle and Late Life* (New York: Atherton, 1964), 125–30, 135–7.

    6. Theoretical discussions can be found in: C. Adams, G. Labouvie-Vief, C. J. Hobart, and M. Dorosz, "Adult Age Group Differences in Story Recall Style," manuscript in review; and G. Labouvie-Vief, J. Hakim-Larson, and M. DeVoe, "The Language of Self-Regulation: A Life-Span View," manuscript in review. Empirical studies include, among others: A. Chinen, A. Spielvogel, and D. Farrell, "The Experience of Intuition," *Psychological Perspectives* 16 (1985): 186–209; N. Kogan, "Categorizing and Conceptualizing Styles in Younger and Older Adults," *Human Development* 17 (1974): 218–230; and K. Waddell and B. Rogoff, "Effect of Contextual Organization on Spatial Memory of Middle-aged and Older Women," *Developmental Psychology* 17 (1981): 878–85.

    7. M. Buber, *I and Thou*, trans. W. Kaufmann (New York: Scribner's, 1970), 56–7.

    8. Else Frenkel, "Studies in Biographical Psychology," *Character and Personality* 5 (1936): 8–9; E. Erikson, J. M. Erickson, and H. Q. Kivnick, *Vital Involvement in Old Age* (New York: Norton, 1986), 225. As noted before, the "late style" of great artists often reflects a numinous sense of wonder—see H. Munsterberg, *The Crown of Life* (New York: Harcourt Brace Jovanovich, 1983), 7–8, 21, 24–5, 29, 32.

    The emergence of mystical experiences in later life can be observed more dramatically in other cultures more accepting of spirituality. See M. Biesele and N. Howell, "The Old People Give You Life," in P. T. Amoss and S. Harrell, eds., *Other Ways of Growing Old* (Palo Alto, Calif.: Stanford University Press, 1981), 91. See also K. Sinclair, "Maori Women at Midlife," in J. K. Brown and V. Kerns, eds., *In Her Prime* (South Hadley, Mass.: Bergin and Garvey, 1985), 128.

9. This is the distinction between "pre-personal" and "transpersonal" experiences. The former involves a person who has not yet developed adequate ego-functioning, i.e., a sturdy sense of self, the ability to modulate instincts, and the capacity to separate reality from fantasy. "Transpersonal" experiences involve mystical, intuitive or altered states of consciousness in a person who has adequate ego-functioning, and who can therefore integrate these extraordinary episodes with the demands of human society and everyday life. See K. Wilber, *No Boundary: Eastern and Western Approaches to Personal Growth* (Boston: Shambhala, 1981).

10. F. Arnstein, *Time Out of Mind* (San Francisco: Cragmont, 1986). By permission from the author.

11. A. Kornhaber and K. Woodward, *Grandparents/Grandchildren: The Vital Connection* (Garden City: Doubleday, 1981), 54.

12. O. G. Brim, "Theories of the Male Mid-life Crisis," *Counseling Psychologist* 6 (1976): 2 – 9; E. B. Palmore and D. Maeda, *The Honorable Elders Revisited* (Durham: Duke University Press, 1986), 15; B. J. Horacek, "Life Review: A Pastoral Counseling Technique," in J. A. Thorson, and T. C. Cook, eds., *Spiritual Well-Being of the Elderly* (Springfield, Ill.: Charles C. Thomas, 1978), 105; P. Pruyser, "Aging: Downward, Upward or Forward?" *Pastoral Psychology* 24 (1975): 102 – 18; M. Thurnher, "Continuities and Discontinuities in Values," in M. F. Lowenthal, M. Thurnher, and D. Chiriboga, eds., *Four Stages of Life* (San Francisco: Jossey Bass, 1975), 187, 192; P. Mussen and N. Haan, "A Longitudinal Study of Patterns of Personality and Political Ideologies," in D. Eichorn, *Present and Past in Middle Life* (New York: Academic Press, 1981), 403.

13. R. Guardini, "The Stages of Life and Philosophy," *Philosophy Today* (1957): 78 – 9.

14. P. Cameron, K. G. Desai, D. Bahador, and G. Dremel, "Temporality Across the Life-span," *International Journal of Aging and Human Development* 8 (1977 – 8): 229 – 59; W. Clements, "The Sense of Life Time in Human Development," *Journal of Religion and Health* 18 (1979): 88 – 92.

15. A. B. Chinen, "Eastern Wisdom, Western Aging," paper presented at the Gerontological Society, San Antonio, 1984.

16. M. Grotjahn, "The Day I Got Old," *Psychiatric Clinics of North America* 5 (1982): 234.

17. Comparative discussions on "enlightenment" and mystical experience can be found in: B. Scharfstein, *Mystical Experience* (Baltimore: Penguin, 1974); F. Staal, *Exploring Mysticism* (Berkeley: University of California Press, 1975); and John White, ed., *The Highest State of Consciousness* (New York: Anchor, 1972), especially chapters 6, 15, 16 and 31.

Jung and Maslow implicitly linked enlightenment and maturation. Jung, for instance, interpreted enlightenment as the integration of ego and Self, which was the goal of individuation in the second half of life. See "Foreword to 'An Introduction to Zen Buddhism,' " (1939) in *Collected Works,* vol. 11 (Princeton: Princeton University Press, 1958) para. 884 – 8, 903 – 4, 906; Maslow, in turn, studied self-actualizing individuals and found that all the subjects who qualified were over 50. See *Toward a Psychology of Being* (New York: Van Nostrand, 1968), and *Motivation and Personality* (New York: Harper and Row, 1970).

An explicit discussion of enlightenment and maturation can be found in M. Washburn, *The Ego and the Dynamic Ground* (Albany, N.Y.: State University of New York Press, 1988), especially chapter 9.

18. Z. Shibayama, *A Flower Does Not Talk* (Tokyo: Tuttle, 1970), 205.

19. See, for instance, W. T. Stace, *Teachings of the Mystic* (New York: Mentor, 1960), 40, 45; W. James, *The Varieties of Religious Experience* (1902; reprint, New York: Mentor, 1958), 174, 183,199; and L. Hixon, *Coming Home: the Experience of Enlightenment in Sacred Traditions* (New York: Anchor, 1978), 52, 107, 127, 129, 132, 137 – 40, 142.

20. The increasing rarity of "higher" developmental levels has been found in the domain of moral, religious, and ego development. S. R. Cook, "Stage 5, 5/6, and 6 in Loevinger's Ego Developmental Sequence: An Analysis," paper presented to the Second Symposium on Post-formal Operations, Harvard University, 1985; J. Fowler, *The Stages of Faith* (San Francisco: Harper and Row, 1981), 200; L. Kohlberg and R. Ryncarz, "The Question of Stage Six," paper presented to the Second Symposium on Post-formal Operations, Harvard University, 1985; G. Labouvie-Vief, J. Hakim-Larson, and D. Hobart, "Age, Ego Level and the Life-span Development of Coping and Defense Processes," *Psychology and Aging* 2 (1987): 286 – 93.

Chapter 13

1. M. L. Von Franz, *Redemption Motifs in Fairy Tales* (Toronto: Inner City Books, 1980), 70; D. L. Miller, "Fairy Tale or Myth," in *Spring 1976* (Dallas: Spring Publications, 1976) 157 – 64; cf. B. Bettelheim, *Uses of Enchantment* (New York: Knopf, 1976), 289, who focuses only on sexual symbolism, and J. Heuscher, *Psychiatric Study of Myths and Fairy Tales* (Springfield, Ill.: Charles C. Thomas, 1974), 234 – 6, who discusses both the sexual and transformational symbolism.

2. A. Lang, *The Brown Fairy Book* (London: Longmans, Green, 1914); Y. T. Ozaki, *The Japanese Fairy Book* (Tokyo: Tuttle, 1970).

3. M. Biesele and N. Howell, "The Old People Give You Life," in P. T. Amoss and S. Harrell, eds., *Other Ways of Growing Old* (Palo Alto, Calif.: Stanford University Press, 1981), 89 – 90; A. Holmberg, "Age in the Andes," in Robert Kleemeier, ed., *Aging and Leisure* (New York: Oxford University Press, 1961), 89; J. Nason, "Respected Elder or Old Person: Aging in a Micronesian Community," in P. T. Amoss and S. Harrell, eds., *Other Ways of Growing Old,* 163; C. Rustom, "The Later Years of Life and the Use of Time Among the Burmans," in R. Kleemeier, ed., *Aging and Leisure;* M. N. Shahrani, "Growing in Respect: Aging Among the Kirghiz of Afghanistan," in P. T. Amoss and S. Harrell, eds., *Other Ways of Growing Old,* 189 – 90.

4. D. Gutmann, "Observations on Culture and Mental Health in Later Life,"

in J. Birren and R. B. Sloane, eds., *Handbook of Mental Health and Aging* (New York: Prentice-Hall, 1983), 433.

5. J. Kotre, *Outliving the Self: Generativity and the Interpretation of Lives* (Baltimore: Johns Hopkins University Press, 1984), 116.

6. Biesele and Howell, "The Old People Give You Life," 89, 96; H. Sharp, "Old Age Among the Chipweyan," in P. T. Amoss and S. Harrell, eds., *Other Ways of Growing Old,* 106 – 7; A. Holmberg, "Age in the Andes," in Robert Kleemeier, ed., *Aging and Leisure,* 89; C. C. Hughes, "The Concept and Use of Time in the Middle-years: The St. Lawrence Island Eskimos," in R. Kleemeier, ed., *Aging and Leisure,* 93.

Secular versions of the grandparents' mediating role can be found in American culture. S. Cath, "Clinical Vignettes: A Range of Grandparenthood Experiences," *Journal of Geriatric Psychiatry* 19 (1986): 57 – 68; M. Crawford, "Not Disengaged: Grandparents in Literature and Reality, An Empirical Study in Role Satisfaction," *Sociological Review* 29 (1981): 499 – 519; P. Gorlitz and D. Gutmann, "The Psychological Transition into Grandparenthood," in J. G. Howells, ed., *Modern Perspectives in the Psychiatry of Middle Age* (New York: Bruner/Mazel, 1981); A. Kornhaber and K. Woodward, *Grandparents/Grandchildren: The Vital Connection* (Garden City: Doubleday, 1981), 130.

7. Kornhaber and Woodward, *Grandparents/Grandchildren,* xxiv – xxv, 110.

8. Fairy tales are clear about this point: in many stories, a young man or woman receives a magic gift—three wishes in the Grimms' tale "The Fisherman and His Wife," and the power to heal in their tale "The Godfather." Without the advice of a wise old figure, they abuse their gifts and bring disaster upon themselves.

9. S. de Beauvoir, *The Coming of Age,* trans. P. O'Brian (New York: G.P. Putnams' Sons, 1972), 66; M. Biesele and N. Howell, "The Old People Give You Life," 92; J. Nason, "Aging in a Micronesian Community," 164 – 5.

Chapter 14

1. The succession of objects the old man hauls up can be interpreted in a variety of ways. The jackass, for instance, is a beast of burden, and so can be interpreted as a symbol of labor. We saw the same motif in "Fortune and the Woodcutter," where the mules are the key to fortune falling into the woodcutter's lap. (The Grimms' fable "The Duration of Life" provides a similar association. The ass, the dog, and the monkey asked God to take away several years from their normal life span, because they did not wish to linger in old age. God then gave man 30 years, but man complained it was too little. So God gave man the donkey's extra years. Man was still unsatisfied. So God added on the dog's years, and then the monkey's. Thus man enjoys the first thirty years of life, healthy and happy. Then he lives like a jackass, with burden after burden placed upon him, later like an old dog, growling and toothless, and finally, like a foolish monkey.) If the jackass symbolizes responsibility and work, the fact that it is dead in the present tale suggests that the old man's psychological task does not involve dedication and duty, as it would for a younger protagonist. As something dead and decaying, the carcass of

the jackass also makes a good symbol for the shadowy side of human nature—all the unsavory things men do or think.

The second thing the old man hauls up is a pot filled with sand. Pots are used to store things (like the old man's pennies in "The Simple Grasscutter") and so can be interpreted as a symbol of saving, especially for old age. Here, however, the pot is filled with sand, suggesting that material wealth is not the issue. Finally, the fisherman dredges up potsherds, connoting death and destruction.

2. R. Otto, *The Idea of the Holy* (1917; reprint, London: Oxford University Press, 1950); cf. a clinical psychological approach to numinousity, N. Schwartz-Salant, *Narcissism and Character Transformation* (Toronto: Inner City Books, 1982), 16.

3. D. A. Boswell, "Metaphoric Processing in the Mature Years," *Human Development* 22 (1979): 373–84; C. Adams, M. Dorosz, C. Holmes, S. Bass, D. Gossiaux, and G. Labouvie-Vief, "Qualitative Age Differences in Story Recall," unpublished manuscript in review; G. Labouvie-Vief, D. A. Schell, and S. E. Weaverdyck, "Recall Deficit in the Aged: A Fable Recalled," in press; G. Lavouvie-Vief, S. O. Campbell, S. E. Weaverdyck, and M. K. Tanenhaus, "Metaphoric Processing in Young and Old Adults," in press; C. Dent, "The Development of Metaphoric Competence: a symposium," *Human Development* 29 (1986): 223–44.

4. J. Kotre, *Outliving the Self* (Baltimore: Johns Hopkins University Press, 1984), 227ff, 251ff. Dieckmann, in his book, *Twice-Told Tales: the Psychological Use of Fairy Tales* (Wilmette, Ill.: Chiron Publications, 1986), discusses similar examples from his clinical practice.

5. C. G. Jung, "The Symbolism of the Mandala" (1944), *Collected Works*, vol. 12 (Princeton: Princeton University Press, 1953), especially para. 316, 327–8.

6. C. G. Jung, "Marriage as a Psychological Relationship" (1925), in *Collected Works* vol. 17 (Princeton: Princeton University Press, 1954), para 331a; and "The Psychology of the Unconscious" (1943), in *Collected Works* Vol. 7 (Princeton: Princeton University Press, 1953), para 88–91; E. Frenkel, "Studies in Biographical Psychology," *Character and Personality* 5 (1936): 8; P. Cameron, "Introversion and Egocentricity Among the Aged," *Journal of Gerontology* 22 (1967): 465p–8; B. Neugarten and D. Miller, "Ego Functions in the Middle and Later Years: A Further Exploration," in B. L. Neugarten, ed., *Personality in Middle and Late Life: Empirical Studies* (New York: Atherton, 1964), 99; A. Van Kaam, *The Transcendent Self: Formative Spirituality of the Middle, Early and Later Years of Life* (Denville, N.J.: Dimension Books, 1979), 109ff.

7. E. Erikson, J. M. Erikson, and H. Q. Kivnick, *Vital Involvement in Old Age* (New York: Norton, 1986), 74; Kotre, *Outliving the Self*, 116ff; A. Kornhaber and K. Woodward, *Grandparents/Grandchildren: The Vital Connection* (Garden City: Doubleday, 1981), 74.

8. P. Pruyser, "Aging: Upward, Downward or Forward?" *Pastoral Psychology* 24 (1975): 115–6; J. McLeish, *The Ulyssean Adult: Creativity in the Middle and Later Years* (New York: McGraw-Hill Ryerson, 1976), 16ff, 197ff, 229.

9. S. de Beavoir, *The Coming of Age*, trans. P. O'Brian (New York: G. P. Putnam's Sons, 1972), 489ff.

10. E. B. Palmore and D. Maeda, *The Honorable Elders Revisited* (Durham: Duke University Press, 1986), 94.

11. Bruno Bettelheim, *Uses of Enchantment* (New York: Knopf, 1976), 28–34.

12. J. Zipes, *Don't Bet on the Prince: Contemporary Feminist Fairy Tales in North America and England* (New York: Methuen, 1986), 6–7; *Fairy Tales and the Art of Subversion: The Classical Genre for Children and the Process of Socialization* (New York: Heinemann, 1983), 6ff, 47ff; *Breaking the Magic Spell: Radical Theories of Folk and Fairy Tales* (Austin: University of Texas Press, 1979), 3, 5, 8; M. Tatar, *The Hard Facts of the Grimms' Fairy Tales* (Princeton: Princeton University Press, 1987), 19ff.

The Grimms' tale "Spirit in a Bottle" resembles the "Fisherman and the Djinn" closely, except that the protagonist is a child rather than an old man, and there is no liberation of society. Indeed, the Grimms' story may derive from the Arabian one, since the "Thousand and One Nights" was known to medieval Europe. Such historical connections are difficult to prove, but if true, it would provide an earlier precedent for Bettelheim's inadvertent editing, diminishing the elder's role in fairy tales in favor of children.

13. A. B. Chinen, "Middle Tales: Fairy Tales and Transpersonal Development at Midlife," *Journal of Transpersonal Psychology* 19 (1987): 99–132.

14. M. Tatar notes an intriguing similarity between the European tale of Bluebeard, and the frame story of the Arabian Nights; *The Hard Facts of the Grimms' Fairy Tales* (Princeton: Princeton University Press, 1987), 167. Both tales involve a married man who kills all his wives. Tatar speculates that the European story is derived from the Arabian one (analogous to the possible derivation of "Spirit in a Bottle" from "The Fisherman and the Djinn"). If true, the Bluebeard story provides another example of how the psychology of later life was eliminated in European tales. In the original Arabian tale, the murderous husband reforms his ways, as the result of Scheherazade's 1001 tales. This theme of self-reformation is totally absent in the European version, where Bluebeard simply murders his latest wife.

15. J. Campbell, "Folkloristic Commentary," in J. Grimm, *The Complete Grimms' Fairy Tales*, trans. M. Hunt (New York: Pantheon, 1944), 846ff.

16. This is a point that otherwise contentious folklorists agree on. See: J. Campbell, "Folkloristic Commentary," 847–64; S. S. Jones, "The Structure of Snow White," in R. Bottigheimer, ed., *Fairy Tales and Society: Illusion, Allusion and Paradigm* (Philadelphia: University of Pennsylvania Press, 1986) 181; M. Luthi, *The Fairy Tale as Art Form and Portrait of Man*, trans. J. Erickson (Bloomington, Ind.: Indiana University Press, 1984), 165ff; J. Zipes, *Fairy Tales and the Art of Subversion*, 165ff.

Chapter 15

1. S. de Beauvoir, *The Coming of Age*, trans. P. O'Brian (New York: G. P. Putnam's Sons, 1972), 84–5, 207. The unflattering comparison of infirm old people with children is found across cultures. In Micronesia, for instance, the same word, "fitigogo," is applied to irresponsible children and incompetent old people—

J. D. Nason, "Aging in a Micronesian Community," in P. T. Amoss and S. Harrell, eds., *Other Ways of Growing Old* (Palo Alto, Calif.: Stanford University Press, 1981), 164.

2. J. E. Spar, "Dementia in the Aged," *Psychiatric Clinics of North America* 5 (1982): 67 – 86; M. E. Linden, "Regression and Recession in the Psychoses of the Aging," in N. E. Zinberg and I. Kaufman, eds., *Normal Psychology of the Aging Process* (New York: International Universities Press, 1963), 137.

3. D. E. Papalia and D. D. Bielby, "Cognitive Functioning in Middle and Old Age Adults: A Review of Research Based on Piaget's Theory," *Human Development* 17 (1974): 424 – 43; D. B. Bromley, "Studies of Intellectual Function in Relation to Age and Their Significance for Professional and Managerial Functions," *Interdisciplinary Topics in Gerontology* 4 (1969): 103 – 26; F. Craik, "Age Differences in Human Memory," in J. E. Birren and K. W. Schaie, *Handbook of the Psychology of Aging*, 606 – 25.

4. M. Berezin, "Some Intrapsychic Aspects of Aging," in N. E. Zinberg and I. Kaufman, eds., *Normal Psychology of the Aging Process* (New York: International Universities Press, 1961), 93 – 117; M. Grotjahn, "Some Analytic Observations About the Process of Growing Old," *Psychoanalysis and the Social Sciences* 3 (1951): 301 – 12; M. E. Linden, "Regression and Recession in the Psychoses of the Aging," in N. E. Zinberg and I. Kaufman, eds., *Normal Psychology of the Aging Process*, 137; J. Meerloo, "Geriatric Psychotherapy," *Acta Psychotherapeutica et Psychosomatica* 9 (1961): 169 – 82.

5. S. Freud, *Complete Introductory Lectures to Psychoanalysis*, trans. J. Strachey (New York: Norton, 1966), 562ff.

6. C. Malatesta, "Affective Development Over the Lifespan," *Merrill-Palmer Quarterly* 27 (1981): 157ff; D. Gutmann, "An Exploration of Ego Configurations in Middle and Later Life," in B. L. Neugarten, ed., *Personality in Middle and Late Life: Empirical Studies* (New York: Atherton, 1964), 129, 145ff.

7. J. E. Birren, "Age and Decision Strategies," *Interdisciplinary Topics in Gerontology* 4 (1969): 23 – 36; G. Labouvie-Vief, "Action, Concept and Adaptation: A Postformal Theory of Development," paper presented to the Second Symposium on Post-formal Operations, Harvard University, 1985.

J. Sinnott, "A Model for Solution of Ill-structured Problems: Implications for Everyday and Abstract Problem Solving," paper presented to the Gerontological Society, San Antonio, 1984; "Individuals' Strategies in Everyday Problem Solving: Noncognitive and Cognitive Parameters," paper presented to the Gerontological Society, San Francisco, 1983; "Lifespan Relativistic Postformal Thought: Methodology and Data from Everyday Problem-Solving Studies," in M. L. Commons, J. D. Sinnott, F. A. Richards, and C. Armon, eds., *Beyond Formal Operations. Volume 2: Comparisons and Applications of Adolescent and Adult Developmental Models* (New York: Praeger, in press).

8. A. Chinen, A. Spielvogel, and D. Farrell, "The Experience of Intuition," *Psychological Perspectives* 16 (1985): 186 – 209; G. Labouvie-Vief, "Models of Knowledge and Organization of Development," in M. L. Commons, C. Armon, L. Kohlberg, F. A. Richards, T. Grotzer, and J. D. Sinnott, *Beyond Formal Operations.*

173

Volume 3: Models and Methods in the Study of Adolescent and Adult Thought (New York: Praeger, in press).

9. Quoted in de Beauvoir, *The Coming of Age*, 370. See also 372, 486.

10. W. Baylin, S. K. Gordon, and M. F. Nehrke, "Reminiscing and Ego Integrity in Institutionalized Elderly Males," *Gerontologist* 16 (1976): 118 – 24; R. N. Butler, "The Life Review: An Interpretation of Reminiscence in the Aged," *Psychiatry* 26 (1963): 63 – 76; B. J. Hateley, "Spiritual Well-being Through Life Histories," paper presented at the Gerontological Society of America, Annual Meeting, San Francisco, 1983.

11. D. Gutmann, "The Post-parental Years: Clinical Problems and Developmental Possibilities," in W. Norman and T. Scaramella, eds., *Mid-life: Developmental and Clinical Issues* (New York: Brunner/Mazel, 1980), 45; J. Kotre, *Outliving the Self* (Baltimore: Johns Hopkins University Press, 1984), 116 – 7, 227ff; J. Meerloo, "Geriatric Psychotherapy," *Acta Psychotherapeutica* 9 (1961): 169 – 82.

12. M. Biesele and N. Howell, "The Old People Give You Life," in P. T. Amoss and S. Harrell, eds., *Other Ways of Growing Old*, 89; A. Kornhaber and K. Woodward, *Grandparents/Grandchildren: The Vital Connection* (Garden City: Doubleday, 1981), 149 – 50.

Chapter 16

1. T. H. Holmes and R. H. Rahe, "The Social Readjustment Rating Scale," *Journal of Psychosomatic Research* 11 (1967): 213 – 18.

2. E. Neumann, *The Origins and History of Consciousness* (Princeton: Princeton University Press, 1954), 255. Cf. M. Luthi, *The Fairy Tale as Art Form and Portrait of Man*, trans. J. Erickson (Bloomington, Ind.: Indiana University Press, 1984), 15.

3. M. L. Von Franz, *Individuation in Fairy Tales* (Dallas: Spring Publications, 1977), 150; Neumann, *Origins and History of Consciousness*, 71.

4. D. L. Miller, "Fairy Tale or Myth," in *Spring 1976* (Dallas: Spring Publications, 1976), 159.

5. F. Hyde-Chambers and A. Hyde-Chambers, *Tibetan Folk Tales* (Boulder, Col.: Shambhala, 1981), 186.

6. The story also says the old man hangs the fish from the rafters of his house. This conjures up images of hanging from wooden beams, and thus offers an indirect metaphor for the crucifixion of Christ, hanging from the symbolic tree of life.

Chapter 17

1. The heroic paradigm is well summarized by J. Campbell, *The Hero with a Thousand Faces* (Princeton: Princeton University Press, 1949). See also M. Luthi, *The Fairy Tale as Art Form and Portrait of Man*, trans. J. Erickson (Bloomington, Ind.: Indiana University Press, 1984), 165ff. M. Tatar offers a new viewpoint in her article, "Born Yesterday: Heroes in the Grimms' Fairy Tales," in R. Bottigheimer, ed., *Fairy Tales and Society: Illusion, Allusion and Paradigm* (Philadelphia: University of Pennsylvania Press, 1986), 95 – 114.

2. W. Lederer and A. Botwin insist that a greater emphasis on the hero archetype is needed. See their article, "Where Have All the Heros Gone? Another View of Changing Masculine Roles," in K. Solomon and N. Levy, eds., *Men In Transition: Theory and Therapy* (New York: Plenum, 1982), 241 – 6.

Bibliography

Adams, C.; Labouvie-Vief, G.; Hobart, C. J.; and Dorosz, M. "Adult Age Group Differences in Story Recall Style." Unpublished manuscript in review.

Adams, C.; Dorosz, M.; Holmes, C.; Bass, S.; Gossiaux, D.; and Labouvie-Vief, G. "Qualitative Age Differences in Story Recall." Unpublished manuscript in review.

Afanasev, A. N. *Russian Fairy Tales.* New York: Pantheon, 1945.

Amoss, P. T., and Harrell, S. "An Anthropological Perspective." In *Other Ways of Growing Old,* edited by P. Amoss and S. Harrell, pp. 1 – 24. Palo Alto, Calif.: Stanford University Press, 1981.

Anshin, R. "Creativity, Mid-life Crisis and Herman Hesse." *Journal of the American Academy of Psychoanalysis* 4 (1976): 215 – 26.

Arnett, W. S. "Only the Bad Died Young in the Ancient Middle East." *International Journal of Aging and Human Development* 21 (1985): 155 – 60.

Arnstein, F. *Time Out of Mind.* San Francisco: Cragmont, 1986.

Assagioli, R. *The Act of Will.* Baltimore: Penguin, 1974.

––––––. *Psychosynthesis: A Manual of Principles and Techniques.* New York: Hobbs, Dorman, 1965.

Ausubel, N. *A Treasury of Jewish Folklore: Stories, Traditions, Legends, Humor, Wisdom and Folk Songs of the Jewish People.* New York: Crown, 1948.

Bain, R. N. *Cossack Fairy Tales and Folk Tales.* New York: Stokes, 1895.

Baker, B. and Wheelwright, J. "Analysis with the Aged." In *Jungian Analysis,* edited by M. Stein, pp. 256 – 74. La Salle, Ill., and London: Open Court, 1982.

Baylin, W.; Gordon, S. K.; Nehrke, M. F. "Reminiscing and Ego Integrity in Institutionalized Elderly Males." *Gerontologist* 16 (1976): 118 – 24.

de Beauvoir, S. *The Coming of Age.* Translated by P. O'Brian. New York: G. P. Putnam's Sons, 1972.

Berezin, M. "Some Intrapsychic Aspects of Aging." In *Normal Psychology of the Aging Process,* edited by N. E. Zinberg and I. Kaufman, pp. 93 – 117. New York: International Universities Press, 1961.

Berlic-Mazuranic, I. *Croatian Tales of Long Ago.* London: Allen and Unwin, 1924.

Berman, M. *The Re-enchantment of the World.* Ithaca, N.Y.: Cornell University Press, 1981.

Bettelheim, B. *The Uses of Enchantment: The Meaning and Importance of Fairy Tales.* New York: Knopf, 1976.

Bianchi, E. C. *Aging as a Spiritual Journey.* New York: Crossroads, 1984.

Biesele, M., and Howell, N. " 'The Old People Give You Life': Aging Among !Kung Hunter-Gatherers." In *Other Ways of Growing Old,* edited by P. Amoss and S. Harrell, pp. 77 – 98. Palo Alto, Calif.: Stanford University Press, 1981.

Birren, J. "Age and Decision Strategies." *Interdisciplinary Topics in Gerontology* 4 (1969): 23 – 36.

Blazer, D. *Depression in Later Life.* St. Louis: Mosby, 1982.

Block, J. "Psychological Development of Female Children and Adolescents." In

Women: A Developmental Perspective, edited by P. W. Berman and E. R. Ramey, pp. 107 – 24. Washington, D.C.: National Institutes of Health, 1982.

Block, M.; Davidson, J.; and Grambs, J. *Women Over Forty: Visions and Realities.* New York: Springer, 1981.

Blos, P. *On Adolescence: A Psychoanalytic Interpretation.* New York: Free Press, 1966.

Boles, J., and Tatro, C. "Androgyny." In *Men In Transition: Theory and Therapy,* edited by K. Solomon and N. Levy, pp. 99 – 130. New York: Plenum, 1982.

Boswell, D. A. "Metaphoric Processing in the Mature Years." *Human Development* 22 (1979): 373 – 84.

Brewi, J., and Brennan, A. *Mid-life: Psychological and Spiritual Perspectives.* New York: Crossroads, 1985.

Brim, O. G. "Theories of the Male Mid-life Crisis." *Counseling Psycholoigst* 6 (1976): 2 – 9.

Brink, T. "Geriatric Depression and Hypochondriasis: Incidence, Interaction, Assessment and Treatment." *Psychotherapy: Theory, Research and Practice* 19 (1982): 506 – 11.

Brockett, E. *Burmese and Thai Fairy Tales.* London: Frederick Muller, 1965.

Bromley, D. B. "Studies of Intellectual Functioning in Relation to Age and Their Significance for Professional and Managerial Functions." *Interdisciplinary Topics in Gerontology* 4 (1969): 103 – 26.

Brooks, J. B. "Social Maturity in Middle Age and Its Developmental Antecedents." In *Present and Past in Middle Life,* edited by D. Eichorn, J. Clausen, N. Haan, M. Honzik, and P. Mussen, pp. 244 – 69. New York: Academic Press, 1981.

Brown, P. "Religious Needs of Older Persons." In *Spiritual Well-being of the Elderly,* edited by J. Thorson and T. Cook, pp. 76 – 82. Springfield, Ill.: Charles C. Thomas, 1980.

Browning, D., "Preface To a Practical Theology of Aging." *Pastoral Psychology* 24 (1976): 151 – 67.

Buber, M. *I and Thou.* Translated by W. Kaufmann. New York: Scribner's, 1970.

Buesching, R. "Successful Aging: A Religious Viewpoint." In *Aging: Its Challenge to the Individual and to Society,* edited by W. C. Bier, pp. 282 – 92. New York: Fordham University Press, 1973.

Buhler, C. "The General Structure of the Human Life Cycle." In *The Course of Human Life: A Study of Goals in the Humanistic Perspective,* edited by C. Buhler and F. Massarik, pp. 12 – 26. New York: Springer, 1968.

Burton, R. F., trans. *Tales from the Arabian Nights.* New York: Avenel, 1978.

Butler, R. N. "The Life Review: An Interpretation of Reminiscence in the Aged." *Psychiatry* 26 (1963): 63 – 76.

———. *Why Survive?* New York: Harper and Row, 1975.

Caligiuri, A. "Maturing in the Lord: Reflections on Aging and Spiritual Life." *Studies in Formative Spirituality* 1 (1980): 369 – 78.

Calvino, I. *Italian Folktales.* Translated by G. Martin. New York: Pantheon, 1978.

Cameron, P. "Introversion and Ego-Centricity Among the Aged." *Journal of Gerontology* 22 (1967): 465 – 8.

Cameron, P.; Desai, K. G.; Bahador, D.; and Dremel, G. "Temporality Across the

Life-span." *International Journal of Aging and Human Development* 8 (1977 – 78): 229 – 59.

Campbell, J. "Folkloristic Commentary." In J. Grimm, *The Complete Grimms' Fairy Tales,* pp. 833 – 64. New York: Pantheon, 1944.

——— . *The Hero with a Thousand Faces.* Princeton: Princeton University Press, 1949.

Carp, F. "Senility or Garden-variety Maladjustment?" *Journal of Gerontology* 24 (1969): 203 – 8.

Cath, S. "Clinical Vignettes: A Range of Grandparenthood Experiences." *Journal of Geriatric Psychiatry* 19 (1986): 57 – 68.

Cath, S. "Suicide in the Middle Years: Some Reflections on the Annihilation of the Self." In *Mid-life: Developmental and Clinical Issues,* edited by W. Norman and W. Scaramella, pp. 53 – 72. New York: Brunner/Mazel, 1980.

Chan, W – T. *A Sourcebook in Chinese Philosophy.* Princeton: Princeton University Press, 1963.

Chinen, A. B. "Adult Cognitive Development: The Case of Alfred North Whitehead." In *Beyond Formal Operations. Volume 3: Models and Methods in the Study of Adolescent and Adult Thought,* edited by M. L. Commons, C. Armon, L. Kohlberg, F. A. Richards, T. Grotzer, and J. Sinnott. New York: Praeger. In Press.

——— . "Eastern Wisdom, Western Aging." Paper presented at the Gerontological Society of America, San Antonio, 1984.

——— . "Elder Tales Revisited: Forms of Transcendence in Later Life." *Journal of Transpersonal Psychology* 18 (1986): 171 – 92.

——— . "Elder Tales and Psychological Development in Later Life: A Cross-cultural Hermeneutic Study." *The Gerontologist* 38 (1987): 340 – 6.

——— . "Fairy Tales and Transpersonal Development in Later Life." *Journal of Transpersonal Psychology* 17 (1985): 99 – 122.

——— . "Middle Tales: Fairy Tales and Transpersonal Development at Midlife." *Journal of Transpersonal Psychology* 19 (1987): 99 – 132.

——— . "Modal Logic: A New Paradigm of Adult Development and Late Life Potential." *Human Development* 27 (1984): 42 – 65.

——— . "Self-contexting and Psychotherapy with Older Adults." *Psychotherapy: Theory, Research, Practice* 240 (1986): 411 – 16.

Chinen, A.; Spielvogel, A.; and Farrell, D. "The Experience of Intuition." *Psychological Perspectives* 16 (1985): 186 – 209.

Chiriboga, D., and Thurnher, M. "Concept of Self." In *Four Stages of Life,* edited by M. F. Lowenthal, M. Thurnher, and D. Chiriboga, pp. 62 – 83. San Francisco: Jossey Bass, 1975.

Clausen, J. A. "Men's Occupational Careers in the Middle Years." In *Present and Past in Middle Life,* edited by D. Eichorn, J. Clausen, N. Haan, M. Honzik, and P. Mussen, pp. 231 – 355. New York: Academic Press, 1981.

Clements, W. "The Sense of Life Time in Human Development." *Journal of Religion and Health* 18 (1979): 88 – 92.

Clayton, V. "Erikson's Theory of Human Development as It Applies to the Aged:

Wisdom as Contradictive Cognition." *Human Development* 18 (1975): 119 – 28.

———. "Wisdom and Intelligence: The Nature and Function of Knowledge in the Later Years." *International Journal of Aging and Human Development* 15 (1982): 315 – 22.

Clayton, V., and Birren, J. E. "The Development of Wisdom Across the Life Span: A Reexamination of an Ancient Topic." In *Life-Span Development and Behavior, Volume 3*, edited by P. B. Baltes and O. G. Brim, pp. 103 – 35. New York: Academic Press, 1980.

Cole, T. R. "Aging, Meaning and Well-being: Musings of a Cultural Historian." *International Journal of Aging and Human Development* 19 (1984): 329 – 36.

Colson, E., and Scudder, T. "Old Age in Gwembe District, Zambia." In *Other Ways of Growing Old*, edited by P. Amoss and S. Harrell, pp. 125 – 54. Palo Alto, Calif.: Stanford University Press, 1981.

Cook, S. R. "Stages 5, 5/6, and 6 in Loevinger's Ego Developmental Sequence: An Analysis." Paper presented to the Second Symposium on Post-formal Operations, Harvard Unviersity, 1985.

Counts, D. A. "Tamparonga: 'The Big Women' of Kaliai." In *In Her Prime: A New View of Middle-Aged Women*, edited by J. K. Brown and V. Kerns, pp. 49 – 64. South Hadley, Mass.: Bergin and Garvey, 1985.

Covey, H. C. "Historical Terminology Used to Represent Older People." *The Gerontologist* 28 (1988): 291 – 7.

Craik, F. "Age Differences in Human Memory." In *Handbook of the Psychology of Aging*, edited by M. E. Birren and K. W. Schaie, pp. 384 – 420. New York: Van Nostrand Reinhold, 1977.

Crawford, M. "Not Disengaged: Grandparents in Literature and Reality: An Empirical Study in Role Satisfaction." *Sociological Review* 29 (1981): 499 – 519.

Curran, C. "Aging: A Theological Perspective." In *Aging and the Human Spirit: A Reader in Religion and Gerontology*, edited by C. LeFevre and P. LeFevre, pp. 68 – 82. Chicago: Exploration Press, 1981.

Datan, N. "Midas and Other Mid-life Crises." In *Mid-life: Developmental and Clinical Issues*, edited by W. Norman and W. Scaramella, pp. 3 – 19. New York: Brunner/Mazel, 1980.

———. "The Oedipus Cycle: Developmental Mythology, Greek Tragedy, and the Sociology of Knowledge." Paper presented to the Gerontological Society of America, New Orleans, 1985.

Davidson, L. "Mid-life Crisis in Thomas Mann's *Death in Venice*." Journal of the American Academy of Psychoanalysis 4 (1976): 203 – 14.

De Rivera, J. "Development and the Full Range of Emotion." In *Emotion in Adult Development*, edited by C. Malatesta and C. Izard, pp. 46 – 64. Beverly Hills, Calif.: Sage Publications, 1984.

Degh, L. "Grimm's *Household Tales* and Its Place in the Household: The Social Relevance of a Controversial Classic." In *Fairy Tales as Ways of Knowing: Essays on Marchen in Psychology, Society and Literature*, edited by M. M. Metzger and K. Mommsen, pp. 21 – 53. Bern: Lang, 1982.

Dent, C. "The Development of Metaphoric Competence: A Symposium." *Human Development* 29 (1986): 223 – 44.

Dieckmann, H. *Twice-Told Tales: The Psychological Use of Fairy Tales.* Translated by B. Matthews. Wilmette, Ill.: Chiron Publications, 1986.

Dorson, R. *Folk Legends of Japan.* Tokyo: Tuttle, 1962.

Dundes, A. "Fairy Tales from a Folkloristic Perspective." In *Fairy Tales and Society: Illusion, Allusion and Paradigm,* edited by R. Bottigheimer, pp. 259 – 70. Philadelphia: University of Pennsylvania Press, 1986.

Edinger, E. *The Creation of Consciousness: Jung's Myth for Modern Man.* Toronto: Inner City Books, 1984.

_____ . *Ego and Archetype: Individuation and the Religious Function of the Psyche.* Middlesex, England: Penguin, 1972.

Eliade, M. *Shamanism: Archaic Techniques of Ecstasy.* Translated by W. R. Trask. 1951. Reprint. Princeton: Princeton University Press, 1964.

Emery, G., and Lesher, E. "Treatment of Depression in Older Adults: Personality Considerations." *Psychotherapy: Theory, Research and Practice* 19 (1982): 500 – 5.

Erikson, E. *The Life Cycle Completed.* New York: Norton, 1983.

_____ . *Identity and the Life Cycle.* New York: International Universities Press, 1959.

_____ . "Themes of Adulthood in the Freud-Jung Correspondence." In *Themes of Work and Love in Adulthood,* edited by N. J. Smelser and E. H. Erikson, pp. 43 – 76. Cambridge, Mass.: Harvard University Press, 1980.

Erikson, E.; Erikson, J. M.; and Kivnick, H. Q. *Vital Involvement in Old Age.* New York: Norton, 1986.

Fecher, V. J. *Religion and Aging: An Annotated Bibliography.* San Antonio: Trinity University Press, 1982.

Fowler, J. *The Stages of Faith: The Psychology of Human Development and the Quest for Meaning.* San Francisco: Harper and Row, 1981.

Frenkel, E. "Studies in Biographical Psychology." *Character and Personality* 5 (1936): 1 – 34.

Freud, S. *Complete Introductory Lectures to Psychoanalysis.* Translated by J. Strachey. New York: Norton, 1966.

Friedlander, G. *The Jewish Fairy Book.* New York: Frederick Stokes, 1920.

Funk, J. "Beethoven: A Transpersonal Analysis." *ReVision* 5 (1982): 29 – 41.

_____ . "Music and Fourfold Vision." *ReVision* 6 (1983): 57 – 65.

Gerner, R. H. "Depression in the Elderly." In *Psychopathology of Aging,* edited by O. J. Kaplan. New York: Academic Press, 1979.

Giele, J. Z. "Adulthood as Transcendence of Age and Sex." In *Themes of Work and Love in Adulthood,* edited by N. J. Smelser and E. H. Erikson, pp. 151 – 73. Cambridge, Mass.: Harvard University Press, 1980.

Gilleard, C., and Gurkan, A. "Socioeconomic Development and the Status of Elderly Men in Turkey: A Test of Modernization Theory." *Journal of Gerontology* 42 (1987): 353 – 7.

Gilstrap, R., and Estabrook, I. *The Sultan's Fool and Other North African Tales.* New York: Holt, Rhinehart and Winston, 1958.

Gorlitz, P., and Gutmann, D. "The Psychological Transition into Grandparent-hood." In *Modern Perspectives in the Psychiatry of Middle Age*, edited by J. G. Howells, pp. 167 – 86. New York: Brunner/Mazel, 1981.

Gould, R. "The Phases of Adult Life: A Study in Developmental Psychology." *American Journal of Psychiatry* 29 (1972): 33 – 43.

_____ . *Transformations: Growth and Change in Adult Life.* New York: Simon and Schuster, 1978.

Grimm, J. *The Complete Grimms' Fairy Tales.* Translated by Margaret Hunt. New York: Pantheon, 1944.

Grolnick, S. "Fairy Tales and Psychotherapy." In *Fairy Tales and Society: Illusion, Allusion and Paradigm*, edited by R. Bottigheimer, pp. 203 – 17. Philadelphia: University of Pennsylvania Press, 1986.

Grotjahn, M. "Analytic Psychotherapy with the Elderly." *Psychoanalytic Review* 42 (1955): 419 – 27.

_____ . "The Day I Got Old." *Psychiatric Clinics of North America* 5 (1982): 233 – 5.

_____ . "Some Analytic Observations About the Process of Growing Old." *Psychoanalysis and the Social Sciences* 3 (1951): 301 – 12.

Gruen, W. "Adult Personality: An Empirical Study of Erikson's Theory of Ego Development." In *Personality in Middle and Late Life: Empirical Studies*, edited by B. L. Neugarten, pp. 1 – 14. New York: Atherton, 1964.

Guardini, R. "The Stages of Life and Philosophy." *Philosophy Today* 1 (1957): 78 – 9.

Gurland, B. and Cross, P. "Epidemiology of Psychopathology in Old Age: Some Implications for Clinical Services." *Psychiatric Clinics of North America* 5 (1982): 11 – 26.

Gutmann, D. "The Cross-cultural Perspective: Notes on a Comparative Psychology of Aging." In *Handbook of the Psychology of Aging*, edited by J. Birren and K. W. Schaie, pp. 302 – 29. New York: Van Nostrand Reinhold, 1977.

_____ . "An Exploration of Ego Configurations in Middle and Later Life." In *Personality in Middle and Late Life*, edited by B. L. Neugarten, pp. 114 – 48. New York: Atherton, 1964.

_____ . "Observations on Culture and Mental Health in Later Life." In *Handbook of Mental Health and Aging*, edited by J. E. Birren and R. B. Sloane, pp. 429 – 46. New York: Prentice-Hall, 1983.

_____ . "Psychoanalysis and Aging." In *The Course of Life: Psychoanalytic Contributions Toward Understanding Personality Development. Volume III: Adulthood and the Aging Process*, edited by S. I. Greenspan and G. Pollock, pp. 489 – 517. Washington, D.C.: National Institute of Mental Health, 1981.

_____ . "The Post-Parental Years: Clinical Problems and Developmental Possibilities." In *Mid-life: Developmental and Clinical issues*, edited by W. Norman and T. Scaramella, pp. 38 – 52. New York: Brunner/Mazel, 1980.

Gutmann, D.; Grunes, J.; and Griffing, B. "The Clinical Psychology of Later Life: Developmental Paradigms." In *Transitions in Aging*, edited by N. Datan and N. Lohmann, pp. 119 – 32. New York: Academic Press, 1980.

Haan, N. "Common Dimensions of Personality: Early Adolescence to Middle Life."

In *Present and Past in Middle Life*, edited by D. Eichorn, J. Clausen, N. Haan, M. Honzik, and P. Mussen, pp. 117–54. New York: Academic Press, 1981.

———. "Personality Organization of Well-Functioning Younger People and Older Adults." *International Journal of Aging and Human Development* 7 (1976): 117–27.

Haan, N. and Day, D. "A Longitudinal Study of Change and Sameness in Personality Development." *International Journal of Aging and Human Development* 5 (1974): 11–39.

Harding, M. E. *The Way of All Women: A Psychological Interpretation.* London: Longmans, Green, 1934.

Harrell, S. "Growing Old in Rural Taiwan." In *Other Ways of Growing Old*, edited by P. Amoss and S. Harrell, pp. 193–210. Palo Alto, Calif.: Stanford University Press, 1981.

Hart, D. L. "The Healing Properties of a Fairy Tale." *Psychological Perspectives* 11 (1980): 19–29.

Hateley, B. J. "Spiritual Well-Being Through Life Histories." Paper presented at the Gerontological Society of America, Annual Meeting, San Francisco, 1983.

Heath, D. "The Maturing Person." In *Beyond Health and Normality: Explorations of Exceptional Well-being*, edited by R. Walsh and D. Shapiro, pp. 152–206. New York: Van Nostrand Reinhold, 1983.

Hefner, R.; Rebecca, M.; and Oleshansky, B. "Development of Sex-Role Transcendence." *Human Development* 18 (1975): 142–58.

Henderson, J. *Cultural Attitudes in Psychological Perspective.* Toronto: Inner City Books, 1984.

Heuscher, J. *A Psychiatric Study of Myths and Fairy Tales: Their Origin, Meaning and Usefulness.* Springfield, Ill.: Charles C. Thomas, 1974.

Hiltner, S. *Toward a Theology of Aging.* New York: Human Sciences Press, 1975.

Hixon, L. *Coming Home: The Experience of Enlightenment in Sacred Traditions.* New York: Anchor Books, 1978.

Hodgetts, E. *From the Land of the Tsar.* London: Gilbert and Rivington, 1890.

Holmberg, A. "Age in the Andes." In *Aging and Leisure: A Research Perspective into the Meaningful Use of Time*, edited by R. Kleemeier, pp. 86–90. New York: Oxford University Press, 1961.

Holmes, T. H., and Rahe, R. H. "The Social Readjustment Rating Scale." *Journal of Psychosomatic Research* 11 (1967): 213–18.

Horacek, B. J. "Life Review: A Pastoral Counseling Technique." In *Spiritual Well-Being of the Elderly*, edited by J. A. Thorson and T. C. Cook, pp. 100–7. Springfield, Ill.: Charles C. Thomas, 1978.

Hughes, C. C. "The Concept and Use of Time in the Middle-Years: The St. Lawrence Island Eskimos." In *Aging and Leisure: A Research Perspective into the Meaningful Use of Time*, edited by R. Kleemeier, pp. 91–5. New York: Oxford University Press, 1961.

Hyde-Chambers, F., and Hyde-Chambers, A. *Tibetan Folk Tales.* Boulder, Col.: Shambhala, 1981.

In-Sob, Z., ed. *Folk Tales from Korea.* New York: Grove Press, 1979.

183

Inhelder, B., and Piaget, J. *The Growth of Logical Thinking from Childhood to Adolescence.* New York: Basic Books, 1958.

Jacobs, J. *Indian Fairy Tales.* New York: G. P. Putnam's Sons, 1890.

James, W. *The Varieties of Religious Experience.* 1902. Reprint. New York: Mentor, 1958.

Johnson, R. *He: Understanding Masculine Psychology.* New York: Perennial Library, 1976.

Jones, S. S. "The Structure of Snow White." In *Fairy Tales and Society: Illusion, Allusion and Paradigm,* edited by R. Bottigheimer, pp. 165 – 86. Philadelphia: University of Pennsylvania Press, 1986.

Jung, C. G. 1945. "After the Catastrophe." In *Collected Works,* vol. 10, pp. 194 – 217. Princeton: Princeton University Press, 1964.

_____. 1952. "Answer to Job." In *Collected Works,* vol. 11, pp. 355 – 473. Princeton: Princeton University Press, 1969.

_____. 1939. "Foreword to *An Introduction to Zen Buddhism.*" In *Collected Works,* vol. 11, pp. 538 – 57. Princeton: Princeton University Press, 1969.

_____. 1935. "General Problems of Psychotherapy." In *Collected Works,* vol. 16, pp. 3 – 125. Princeton: Princeton University Press, 1954.

_____. 1925. "Marriage as a Psychological Relationship." In *Collected Works,* vol. 17, pp. 189 – 201. Princeton: Princeton University Press, 1954.

_____. *Memories, Dreams, Reflections.* New York: Pantheon, 1961.

_____. 1943. "The Personal and the Collective Unconscious." In *Collected Works,* vol. 7, pp. 63 – 78. Princeton: Princeton University Press, 1953.

_____. 1921. "Psychological Types." In *Collected Works,* vol. 6, pp. 189 – 201. Princeton: Princeton University Press, 1971.

_____. 1951. "The Psychology of the Child Archetype." In *Collected Works,* vol. 9i, pp. 151 – 81. Princeton: Princeton University Press, 1959.

_____. 1943. "The Psychology of the Unconscious." In *Collected Works,* vol. 7, pp. 3 – 120. Princeton: Princeton University Press, 1953.

_____. 1928. "The Relations between Ego and the Unconscious." In *Collected Works,* vol. 7, pp. 121 – 239. Princeton: Princeton University Press, 1953.

_____. 1931. "The Stages of Life." In *Collected Works,* vol. 8, pp. 387 – 403. Princeton: Princeton University Press, 1960.

_____. 1944. "The Symbolism of the Mandala." In *Collected Works,* vol. 12, pp. 91 – 213. Princeton: Princeton University Press, 1953.

_____. 1952. "Symbols of the Mother and Rebirth." In *Collected Works,* vol. 5, pp. 207 – 73. Princeton: Princeton University Press, 1956.

Jung, E., and Von Franz, M. *The Grail Legend.* Boston: Sigo, 1986.

Kahn, R. I. "Spiritual Well-Being: A Relationship That Nurtures." In *Spiritual Well-Being of the Elderly,* edited by J. A. Thorson and T. C. Cook, Jr., pp. 38 – 50. Springfield, Ill.: Charles C. Thomas, 1978.

Kakar, S. "Setting the Stage: The Traditional Hindu View and the Psychology of Erik H. Erikson." In *Identity and Adulthood,* edited by S. Kakar, pp. 2 – 12. Delhi: Oxford University Press, 1979.

Katz, R. L. "Jewish Values and Socio-Psychological Perspectives on Aging." In

Toward a Theology of Aging, edited by S. Hiltner, pp. 135–50. New York: Human Sciences Press, 1975.

Kernberg, O. *Object Relations Theory and Clinical Psychoanalysis*. New York: Jason Aronson, 1976.

Khan, N. I. *Twenty Jataka Tales*. New York: Inner Traditions International, 1985.

Kielholz, P. *Masked Depression*. Bern: Huber, 1973.

King, K. "Cognition, Metacognition and Epistemic Cognition: A Three-Level Model of Cognitive Processing." *Human Development* 26 (1983): 222–32.

King, P. H. M. "Notes on the Psychoanalysis of Older Patients: Re-appraisal of the Potentialities for Change During the Second Half of Life." *Journal of Analytical Psychology* 19 (1974): 22–37.

King, P. M.; Kitchener, K. S.; Davison, M. L.; Parker, C. A.; and Wood, P. K. "The Justification of Beliefs in Young Adults: A Longitudinal Study." *Human Development* 26 (1983): 106–16.

Kivnick, H. "Grandparenthood and the Life Cycle." *Journal of Geriatric Psychiatry* 19 (1986): 39–56.

Klerman, G. "Problems in the Definition and Diagnosis of Depression in the Elderly." In *Depression and Aging: Causes, Care and Consequences*, edited by L. D. Breslau and M. R. Haug, pp. 3–19. New York: Springer, 1983.

Koenig, H.; Kvale, J.; and Ferrel, C. "Religion and Well-Being in Later Life." *The Gerontologist* 28 (1988): 18–28.

Koenig, H.; George, L.; and Siegler, I. "The Use of Religion and Other Emotion-Regulating Coping Strategies Among Older Adults." *The Gerontologist* 28 (1988): 303–10.

Kogan, N. "Categorizing and Conceptualizing Styles in Younger and Older Adults." *Human Development* 17 (1974): 218–30.

Kohlberg, L. *The Psychology of Moral Development: The Nature and Validity of Moral Stages*. San Francisco: Harper and Row, 1984.

_____. "Stages and Aging in Moral Development—Some Speculations." *The Gerontologist* 13 (1973): 497–502.

Kohlberg, L., and Ryncarz, R. "The Question of Stage Six." Paper presented to the Second Symposium on Post-formal Operations," Harvard University, 1985.

Kornhaber, A. "Grandparenting, Normal and Pathological: A Preliminary Communication from the Grandparent Study." *Journal of Geriatric Psychiatry* 19 (1986): 19–38.

Kornhaber, A., and Woodward, K. *Grandparents/Grandchildren: The Vital Connection*. Garden City: Doubleday, 1981.

Kotre, J. *Outliving the Self: Generativity and the Interpretation of Lives*. Baltimore: Johns Hopkins University Press, 1984.

Kuhlen, R. "Developmental Changes in Motivation During the Adult Years." In *Middle Age and Aging: A Reader in Social Psychology*, edited by B. Neugarten, pp. 115–36. Chicago: University of Chicago Press, 1968.

Laboulaye, E. *Laboulaye's Fairy Book: Fairy Tales of All Nations*. Great Neck, N.Y.: Core, 1976.

Labouvie-Vief, G. "Action, Concept and Adaptation: A Postformal Theory of Development." Paper presented to the Second Symposium on Post-formal Operations, Harvard University, 1985.

――― . "Adaptive Dimensions of Adult Cognition." In *Transitions of Aging*, edited by N. Datan and N. Lohman, pp. 3 – 26. New York: Academic Press, 1980.

――― . "Beyond Formal Operations: The Uses and Limits of Pure Logic in Life-Span Development." *Human Development* 23 (1980): 141 – 61.

――― . "Developmental Dimensions of Adult Adaptation: Perspectives on Mind, Self and Emotion." Symposium presented at the Gerontological Society of America, Chicago, 1986.

――― . "Logic and Self-Regulation from Youth to Maturity: A Model." In *Beyond Formal Operations: Late Adolescent and Adult Cognitive Development*, edited by M. L. Commons, F. A. Richards, and C. Armon, pp. 158 – 80. New York: Praeger, 1984.

――― . "Models of Knowledge and Organization of Development." In *Beyond Formal Operations. Volume 3: Models and Methods in the Study of Adolescent and Adult Thought*, edited by M. L. Commons, C. Armon, L. Kohlberg, F. A. Richards, T. Grotzer, and J. Sinnott. New York: Praeger. In Press.

Lavouvie-Vief, G.; Campbell, S. O.; Weaverdyck, S. E.; and Tanenhaus, M. K. "Metaphoric Processing in Young and Old Adults." Manuscript in review.

Labouvie-Vief, G., and Chandler, M. "Cognitive Development and Life-Span Developmental Theory: Idealistic Versus Contextual Perspectives." In *Life-span Development and Behavior, Volume 1*, edited by P. Baltes, pp. 181 – 210. New York: Academic Press, 1978.

Labouvie-Vief, G.; DeVoe, M.; and Bulka, D. "Speaking About Feelings: Conceptions of Emotion Across the Life Span." Manuscript in review.

Labouvie-Vief, G.; Hakim-Larson, J.; and DeVoe, M. "The Language of Self Regulation: A Life-Span View." Manuscript in review.

Labouvie-Vief, G.; Hakim-Larson, J.; and Hobart, C. "Age, Ego Level and the Life-Span Development of Coping and Defense Processes." *Psychology and Aging* 2 (1987): 286 – 93.

Labouvie-Vief, G.; Schell, D. A.; and Weaverdyck, S. E. "Recall Deficit in the Aged: A Fable Recalled." Manuscript in review.

Lambek, M. "Motherhood and Other Careers in Mayotte." In *In Her Prime: A New View of Middle-Aged Women*, edited by J. K. Brown and V. Kerns, pp. 67 – 86. South Hadley, Mass.: Bergin and Garvey, 1985.

Lang, A. *The Brown Fairy Book*. London: Longmans, Green, 1914.

――― . *The Yellow Fairy Book*. 1894. Reprint. New York: Dover, 1960.

Lawrence, N. *Whitehead's Philosophical Development: A Critical History of the Background of "Process and Reality."* New York: Greenwood Press, 1968.

Lederer, W., and Botwin, A. "Where Have All the Heroes Gone? Another View of Changing Masculine Roles." In *Men In Transition: Theory and Therapy*, edited by K. Solomon and N. Levy, pp. 241 – 6. New York: Plenum, 1982.

Lee, R. B. "Work, Sexuality and Aging Among !Kung Women." In *In Her Prime: A New View of Middle-Aged Women*, edited by J. K. Brown and V. Kerns, pp. 23 – 36. South Hadley, Mass.: Bergin and Garvey, 1985.

LeFevre, C., and LeFevre, P., eds. *Aging and the Human Spirit: A Reader in Religion and Gerontology.* Chicago: Exploration Press, 1981.

Lehman, H. "Affective Disorders in the Aged." *Psychiatric Clinics of North America* 5 (1982): 27–44.

Levinson, D. J.; Darrow, C. N.; Klein, E. B.; Levinson, M. H.; and McKee, B. *The Seasons of a Man's Life.* New York: Ballantine, 1978.

Lewis, R., and Roberts, C. "Postparental Fathers in Distress." In *Men In Transition: Theory and Therapy,* edited by K. Solomon and N. Levy, pp. 199–204. New York: Plenum, 1982.

Lidz, T. "Phases of Adult Life: An Overview." In *Mid-life: Developmental and Clinical Issues,* edited by W. Norman and T. Scaramella, pp. 20–37. New York: Brunner/Mazel, 1980.

Linden, M. E. "Regression and Recession in the Psychoses of the Aging." In *Normal Psychology of the Aging Process,* edited by N. E. Zinberg and I. Kaufman, pp. 125–42. New York: International Universities Press, 1968.

Livson, F. "Paths to Psychological Health in the Middle Years: Sex Differences." In *Present and Past in Middle Life,* edited by D. Eichorn, J. Clausen, N. Haan, M. Honzik, and P. Mussen, pp. 194–221. New York: Academic Press, 1981.

Lowe, V. *Understanding Whitehead.* Baltimore: Johns Hopkins University Press, 1962.

_____ . *Understanding Whitehead: The Man and His Work.* Baltimore: Johns Hopkins University Press, 1985.

Luthi, M. *The Fairy Tale as Art Form and Portrait of Man.* Translated by J. Erickson. Bloomington, Ind.: Indiana University Press, 1984.

_____ . *Once Upon a Time: On the Nature of Fairy Tales.* Bloomington, Ind.: Indiana University Press, 1976.

Maduro, R. "Artistic Creativity and Aging in India." *International Journal of Aging and Human Development* 5 (1975): 303–29.

Maitland, D. J. *Against the Grain: Coming Through the Mid-life Crisis.* New York: Pilgrim Press, 1981.

Malatesta, C. "Affective Development Over the Life-Span: Involution or Growth?" *Merrill-Palmer Quarterly* 27 (1981): 145–73.

Malatesta, C. and Culver, L. "Thematic and Affective Content in the Lives of Adult Women: Patterns of Change and Continuity." In *Emotion in Adult Development,* edited by C. Malatesta and C. Izard, pp. 175–94. Beverly Hills, Calif.: Sage Publications, 1984.

Malatesta, C., and Izard, C. "The Facial Expression of Emotion: Young, Middle-Aged, and Older Adult Expressions." In *Emotion in Adult Development,* edited by C. Malatesta and C. Izard, pp. 253–74. Beverly Hills, Calif.: Sage Publications, 1984.

Manning-Sanders, R. *The Red King and the Witch: Gypsy Folk and Fairy Tales.* New York: Roy, 1964.

Maslow, A. *Motivation and Personality.* New York: Harper and Row, 1970.

_____ . *Toward a Psychology of Being.* New York: Van Nostrand, 1968.

Mayer, F. H. *Ancient Tales in Modern Japan.* Bloomington, Ind.: Indiana University Press, 1985.

187

McAdams, D. "Love, Power, and Images of the Self." In *Emotion in Adult Development*, edited by C. Malatesta and C. Izard, pp. 159–74. Beverly Hills, Calif.: Sage Publications, 1984.

McAllister, T. "Overview: Pseudodementia." *American Journal of Psychiatry* 140 (1983): 528–33.

McLeish, J. *The Ulyssean Adult: Creativity in the Middle and Later Years.* New York: McGraw-Hill Ryerson, 1976.

Meerloo, J. "Geriatric Psychotherapy." *Acta Psychotherapeutica et Psychosomatica* 9 (1961): 169–82.

Mergler, N. L.; Faust, M.; and Goldstein, M. D. "Storytelling as an Age-Dependent Skill." *International Journal of Aging and Human Development* 20 (1984–5): 205–28.

Miller, D. *The New Polytheism: Rebirth of the Gods and Goddesses.* Dallas: Spring Publications, 1981.

———. "Fairy Tale or Myth." In *Spring 1976*, pp. 157–64. Dallas: Spring Publications, 1976.

Mindel, C., and Vaughan, C. "A Multidimensional Approach to Religiosity and Disengagement." *Journal of Gerontology* 33 (1978): 103–8.

Moberg, D. "Religiosity in Old Age." *Gerontologist* 5 (1965): 78–87.

Moss, R. *Chinese Fairy Tales and Fantasies.* New York: Pantheon, 1979.

Munsterberg, H. *The Crown of Life: Artistic Creativity in Old Age.* New York: Harcourt Brace Jovanovich, 1983.

Mussen, P., and Haan, N. "A Longitudinal Study of Patterns of Personality and Political Ideologies." In *Present and Past in Middle Life*, edited by D. Eichorn, J. Clausen, N. Haan, M. Honzik, and P. Mussen, pp. 393–414. New York: Academic Press, 1981.

Myers, J. K.; Weissman, M. M.; Tischler, G. L.; Holzer, C. E.; Leaf, P. J.; and Orvaschel, H. "Six-month Community Prevalence of Psychiatric Disorders in Three Communiteis: 1980–1982." *Archives of General Psychiatry* 41 (Oct. 1984): 959–67.

Nason, J. "Respected Elder or Old Person: Aging in a Micronesian Community." In *Other Ways of Growing Old*, edited by P. Amoss and S. Harrell, pp. 155–74. Palo Alto, Calif.: Stanford University Press, 1981.

Neugarten, B. "Adult Personality: A Developmental View." *Human Development* 9 (1966): 61–73.

———. "Personality and Aging." In *Handbook of the Psychology of Aging*, edited by J. E. Birren and K. W. Schaie, pp. 626–49. New York: Van Nostrand Reinhold, 1977.

Neugarten, B., and Gutmann, D. "Age-Sex Roles and Personality in Middle Age: A Thematic Apperception Study." *Psychological Monographs: General and Applied* 17 (1958): 2–34.

Neugarten, B., and Miller, D. "Ego Functions in the Middle and Later Years: A Further Exploration." In *Personality in Middle and Late Life: Empirical Studies*, edited by B. L. Neugarten, pp. 105–13. New York: Atherton, 1964.

Neumann, E. *The Origins and History of Consciousness.* Princeton: Princeton University Press, 1954.

Newton, P. "Samuel Johnson's Breakdown and Recovery in Middle-Age: A Life-Span Developmental Approach to Mental Illness and Its Cure." *International Review of Psychoanalysis* 11 (1984): 93 – 117.

Nicoloff, A. *Bulgarian Fairy Tales.* Cleveland: Nicoloff, 1979.

Notman, M. "Changing Roles for Women at Mid-Life." In *Midlife: Developmental and Clinical Issues,* edited by W. H. Norman and T. J. Scaramella, pp. 85 – 109. New York: Brunner/Mazel, 1980.

_____ . "Feminine Development: Changes in Psychoanalytic Theory." In *The Woman Patient. Volume 2: Concepts of Femininity and the Life Cycle,* edited by C. Nadelson and M. Notman, pp. 3 – 30. New York: Plenum, 1982.

O'Collins, G. "The Second Journey." *Studies in Formative Spirituality* 1 (1980): 346 – 56.

_____ . *The Second Journey.* New York: Paulist Press, 1978.

Offer, D. O., and Offer, J. B. *From Teenage to Young Manhood: A Psychological Study.* New York: Basic Books, 1976.

Ohta, M. *Japanese Folklore in English.* Tokyo: Miraishi, 1955.

Oser, F., and Reich, K. "The Challenge of Competing Explanations: The Development of Thinking in Terms of Complementarity of 'Theories.' " *Human Development* 30 (1987): 178 – 86.

Otto, R. *The Idea of the Holy.* 1917. Reprint. London: Oxford University Press, 1950.

Ozaki, Y. T. *The Japanese Fairy Book.* Tokyo: Charles Tuttle, 1970.

Palmore, E. B., and Maeda, D. *The Honorable Elders Revisited: A Revised Cross-Cultural Analysis of Aging in Japan.* Durham: Duke Unviersity Press, 1986.

Papalia, D. E., and Bielby, D. D. "Cognitive Functioning in Middle and Old-Age Adults: A Review of Research Based on Piaget's Theory." *Human Development* 17 (1974): 424 – 43.

Pascual-Leone, J. "Attentional, Dialectic and Mental Effort: Toward an Organismic Theory of Life Stages." In *Beyond Formal Operations: Late Adolescent and Adult Cognitive Development,* edited by M. L. Commons, F. A. Richards, and C. Armon, pp. 182 – 215. New York: Praeger, 1984.

Payne, B. P. "Religious Life of the Elderly: Myth or Reality?" In *Spiritual Well-Being of the Elderly,* edited by J. A. Thorson and T. C. Cook, Jr., pp. 218 – 29. Springfield, Ill.: Charles C. Thomas, 1978.

Peck, R. "Psychological Developments in the Second Half of Life." In *Middle Age and Aging: A Reader in Social Psychology,* edited by B. Neugarten, pp. 79 – 83. Chicago: University of Chicago Press, 1968.

Peck, R., and Berkowitz, H. "Personality and Adjustment in Middle Age." In *Personality in Middle and Late Life: Empirical Studies,* edited by B. L. Neugarten, pp. 15 – 43. New York: Atherton, 1964.

Perry, W. G. *Forms of Intellectual and Ethical Development in the College Years.* New York: Holt Rinehart and Winston, 1968.

Piovesana, G. K. "The Aged in Chinese and Japanese Cultures." In *Aging: Its Challenge to the Individual and to Society,* edited by W. C. Bier, pp. 14 – 25. New York: Fordham University Press, 1973.

Powell, P. "Advanced Social Role-Taking and Cognitive Development in Gifted

Adults." *International Journal of Aging and Human Development* 11 (1980): 177 – 92.

Prosen, H.; Martin, R.; and Prosen, M. "The Remembered Mother and the Fanta-sized Mother." *Archives of General Psychiatry* 27 (1972): 791 – 4.

Pruyser, P. "Aging: Downward, Upward or Forward?" *Pastoral Psychology* 24 (1975): 791 – 4.

Rabbit, P. "Changes in Problem Solving Ability in Old Age." In *Handbook of the Psychology of Aging*, edited by J. E. Birren and K. W. Schaie, pp. 606 – 25. New York: Van Nostrand Reinhold, 1977.

Raybeck, D. "A Diminished Dichotomy: Kelantan Malay and Traditional Chinese Perspectives." In *In Her Prime: A New View of Middle-Aged Women*, edited by J. K. Brown and V. Kerns, pp. 155 – 70. South Hadley, Mass.: Bergin and Garvey, 1985.

Raymond, E. F., and Michals, T. J. "Prevalence and Correlates of Depression in Elderly Persons." *Psychological Reports* 47 (1980): 1055 – 61.

Reker, G. T.; Peacock, E. J.; and Wong, T. P. "Meaning and Purpose in Life and Well-Being: A Life-Span Perspective." *Journal of Gerontology* 42 (1987): 43 – 9.

Revere, V., and Tobin, S. "Myth and Reality: The Older Person's Relationship to His Past." *International Journal of Aging and Human Development* 12 (1980): 15 – 26.

Rhadakrishnan, S., and Moore, C. *A Sourcebook in Indian Philosophy.* Princeton: Princeton University Press, 1957.

Rice, D., and Feldman, J. "Living Longer in the United States: Demographic Changes and Health Needs of the Elderly." *Health and Society* 61 (1983): 362 – 71.

Riegel, K. F. "Dialectical Operations: The Final Period of Cognitive Development." *Human Development* 16 (1973): 346 – 70.

Roberts, M. *Chinese Fairy Tales and Fantasies.* New York: Pantheon, 1979.

Rowe, K. "To Spin a Yarn: The Female Voice in Folklore and Fairy Tale." In *Fairy Tales and Society: Illusion, Allusion and Paradigm*, edited by R. Bottigheimer, pp. 53 – 74. Philadelphia: University of Pennsylvania Press, 1986.

Rubin, L. *Women of a Certain Age: The Midlife Search for Self.* New York: Harper and Row, 1979.

Rumnley, D. B., and Bergman, E. "Enchantment and Alchemy: The Story of Rumpelstiltskin." *Bulletin of the Menninger Clinic* 47 (1983): 1 – 14.

Rustom, C. "The Later Years of Life and the Use of Time Among the Burmans." In *Aging and Leisure: A Research Perspective into the Meaningful Use of Time*, edited by R. Kleemeier, pp. 100 – 3. New York: Oxford University Press, 1961.

Rybash, J.; Hoyer, W.; and Roodin, P. *Adult Cognition and Aging; Developmental Changes in Processing, Thinking and Knowing.* Elmsford, N.Y.: Pergamon, 1986.

Sanford, J. *Evil: The Shadow Side of Reality.* New York: Crossroads, 1982.

Scharfstein, B. *Mystical Experience.* Baltimore: Penguin, 1973.

Schenda, R. "Telling Tales—Spreading Tales: Change in the Communicative Forms of a Popular Genre." In *Fairy Tales and Society: Illusion, Allusion and*

Paradigm, edited by R. Bottigheimer, pp. 75 – 94. Philadelphia: University of Pennsylvania Press, 1986.

Schon, D. *The Reflective Practitioner: How Professionals Think in Action.* New York: Basic Books, 1983.

Schwartz-Salant, N. *Narcissism and Character Transformation.* Toronto: Inner City Books, 1982.

Scott-Maxwell, F. *The Measure of My Days.* New York: Penguin, 1968.

Segal, H. "Joseph Conrad and the Mid-Life Crisis." *International Review of Psychoanalysis* 11 (1984): 3 – 9.

Segalla, R. *Departure from Traditional Roles: Mid-Life Women Break the Daisy Chains.* Ann Arbor, Mich.: UMI Research Press, 1982.

Shahrani, M. N. "Growing in Respect: Aging Among the Kirghiz of Afghanistan." In *Other Ways of Growing Old*, edited by P. Amoss and S. Harrell, pp. 175 – 92. Palo Alto, Calif.: Stanford University Press, 1981.

Shainness, N. "Analyzability and Capacity for Change in Middle-Life." *Journal of the American Academy of Psychoanalysis* 7 (1979): 385 – 403.

Sharp, H. "Old Age Among the Chipewyan." In *Other Ways of Growing Old*, edited by P. Amoss and S. Harrell, pp. 99 – 110. Palo Alto, Calif.: Stanford University Press, 1981.

Sheehan, N. W.; Papalia-Finlay, D. E.; and Hooper, F. H. "The Nature of the Life Concept Across the Life-Span." *International Journal of Aging and Human Development* 12 (1981): 1 – 13.

Shibayama, Z. *A Flower Does Not Talk.* Tokyo: Tuttle, 1970.

Silberger, J. "Mourning and Transformation: How Mary Baker Eddy Found in Middle Age a Way of Making a New Life for Herself." *Journal of Geriatric Psychiatry* 12 (1979): 9 – 26.

Simic, A. "Aging in the United States and Yugoslavia: Contrasting Models of Intergenerational Relationships." *Anthropological Quarterly* 50 (1977): 53 – 64.

Simmons, H. "The Quiet Journey: Psychological Journey and Religious Growth from Ages Thirty to Sixty." *Religious Education* 71 (1976): 132 – 42.

Sinclair, K. P. "A Study in Pride and Prejudice: Maori Women at Mid-Life." In *In Her Prime: A New View of Middle-Aged Women*, edited by J. K. Brown and V. Kerns, pp. 117 – 34. South Hadley, Mass.: Bergin and Garvey, 1985.

Sinnott, J. "Individuals' Strategies in Everyday Problem Solving: Noncognitive and Cognitive Parameters." Paper presented to the Gerontological Society, San Francisco, 1983.

––––––. "Lifespan Relativistic Postformal Thought: Methodology and Data from Everyday Problem-Solving Studies." In *Beyond Formal Operations. Volume 2: Comparisons and Applications of Adolescent and Adult Developmental Models*, edited by M. L. Commons, F. A. Richards, and C. Armon. New York: Praeger, in press.

––––––. "A Model for Solution of Ill-Structured Problems: Implications for Everyday and Abstract Problem Solving." Presented to the Gerontological Society, San Antonio, 1984.

––––––. "Postformal Reasoning: The Relativistic Stage." In *Beyond Formal Opera-*

tions: Late Adolescent and Adult Cognitive Development, edited by M. L. Commons, F. A. Richards, and C. Armon, pp. 298–325. New York: Praeger, 1984.

──────. "The Theory of Relativity: A Metatheory for Development." *Human Development* 24 (1981): 293–311.

Sinnott, J., and Guttman, D. "Dialectics of Decision Making in Older Adults." *Human Development* 21 (1978): 190–200.

Smith, R. J. "Japan: The Later Years of Life and the Concept of Time." In *Aging and Leisure: A Research Perspective into the Meaningful Use of Time*, edited by R. Kleemeier, pp. 95–100. New York: Oxford University Press, 1961.

Soddy, K. *Men in Middle Life*. Philadelphia: Lippincott, 1967.

Spar, J. E. "Dementia in the Aged." *Psychiatric Clinics of North America* 5 (1982): 67–86.

Spence, D., and Lurie, E. "Style of Life." In *Four Stages of Life*, edited by M. F. Lowenthal, M. Thurnher, and D. Chiriboga, pp. 1–23. San Francisco: Jossey-Bass, 1975.

Staal, F. *Exploring Mysticism*. Berkeley: University of California Press, 1975.

Stace, W. T. *Teachings of the Mystics*. New York: Mentor, 1960.

Stein, M. *In Midlife*. Dallas: Spring Publications, 1983.

Stroud, J. "Women's Careers: Work, Family and Personality." In *Present and Past in Middle Life*, edited by D. Eichorn, J. Clausen, N. Haan, M. Honzik, and P. Mussen, pp. 356–92. New York: Academic Press, 1981.

Suzuki, D. T. *An Introduction to Zen Buddhism*. New York: Grove Press, 1964.

Swenson, W. M. "Attitudes Toward Death in an Aged Population." *Journal of Gerontology* 16 (1961): 49–52.

Szielzo, C. "An Analysis of Babayaga in Folklore and Fairy Tales." *American Journal of Psychoanalysis* 43 (1983): 167–75.

Tatar, M. "Folkloristic Phantasies: Grimm's Fairy Tales and Freud's Family Romance." In *Fairy Tales as Ways of Knowing: Essays on Märchen in Psychology, Society and Literature*, edited by M. M. Metzger and K. Mommsen, pp. 75–98. Bern: Peter Lang, 1982.

──────. "Born Yesterday: Heroes in the Grimms' Fairy Tales." In *Fairy Tales and Society: Illusion, Allusion and Paradigm*, edited by R. Bottigheimer, pp. 95–114. Philadelphia: University of Pennsylvania Press, 1986.

──────. *The Hard Facts of the Grimms' Fairy Tales*. Princeton: Princeton University Press, 1987.

Tavis, A. "Fairy Tales from a Semiotic Perspective." In *Fairy Tales and Society: Illusion, Allusion and Paradigm*, edited by R. Bottigheimer, pp. 195–202. Philadelphia: University of Pennsylvania Press, 1986.

Thorson J. A., and Cook, T. C. *Spiritual Well-Being of the Elderly*. Springfield, Ill.: Charles C. Thomas, 1978.

Thurnher, M. "Continuities and Discontinuities in Value Orientations." In *Four Stages of Life*, edited by M. F. Lowenthal, M. Thurnher and D. Chiriboga, pp. 176–200. San Francisco: Jossey-Bass, 1975.

──────. "Family Confluence, Conflict and Affect." In *Four Stages of Life*, edited by

M. F. Lowenthal, M. Thurnher, and D. Chiriboga, pp. 24–47. San Francisco: Jossey-Bass, 1975.

Tolkien, J. R. R. *Tree and Leaf.* London: Allen and Unwin, 1976.

Tournier, P. *Learn to Grow Old.* New York: Harper, 1972.

Tseng, W., and Hsu, J. "The Chinese Attitude Toward Parental Authority as Expressed in Children's Stories." *Archives of General Psychiatry* 26 (1972): 28–34.

Turner, B., and Troll, L. "Sex Differences in Psychotherapy with Older People." *Psychotherapy: Theory Research and Practice* 19 (1982): 419–28.

Tzu, L. *The Way of Life.* Translated by R. B. Blakney. New York: New American Library, 1955.

Vaillant, G. *Adaptation to Life: How the Best and the Brightest Came of Age.* Boston: Little, Brown, 1977.

Vaillant, G., and Milofsky, E. "Natural History of Male Psychological Health: IX. Empirical Evidence for Erikson's Model of the Life Cycle." *American Journal of Psychiatry* 137 (1980): 1348–59.

Van Arsdale, P. "The Elderly Asmat of New Guinea." In *Other Ways of Growing Old,* edited by P. Amoss and S. Harrell, pp. 111–24. Palo Alto, Calif.: Stanford University Press, 1981.

Van Kaam, A. *The Transcendent Self: Formative Spirituality of the Middle, Early and Later Years of Life.* Denville, N.J.: Dimension Books, 1979.

Viney, L. "A Sociophenomenological Approach to Life-Span Development Complementing Erikson's Sociodynamic Approach." *Human Development* 30 (1987): 125–36.

Vinson, A. "The Role of Religion in the Maturation of the Autonomous Adult." In *Spiritual Well-Being of the Elderly,* edited by J. A. Thorson and T. C. Cook, Jr., pp. 127–36. Springfield, Ill.: Charles C. Thomas, 1978.

Von Franz, M. L. *Individuation in Fairy Tales.* Dallas: Spring Publications, 1977.

_____ . *The Feminine in Fairy Tales.* Dallas: Spring Publications, 1972.

_____ . *The Psychological Meaning of Redemption Motifs in Fairy Tales.* Toronto: Inner City Books, 1980.

_____ . *Puer Aeternus.* Santa Monica: Sigo, 1970.

_____ . *Shadow and Evil in Fairy Tales.* Dallas, Tex.: Spring Publications, 1974.

Waddell, K., and Rogoff, B. "Effect of Contextual Organization on Spatial Memory of Middle-Aged and Older Women." *Developmental Psychology* 17 (1981): 878–5.

Walsh, R. "The Ten Perfections: Qualities of the Fully Enlightened Individual as Described in Buddhist Psychology." In *Beyond Health and Normality: Explorations of Exceptional Well-being,* edited by R. Walsh and D. Shapiro, pp. 218–28. New York: Van Nostrand Reinhold, 1983.

Washburn, M. *The Ego and the Dynamic Ground.* Albany, N.Y.: State University of New York Press, 1988.

Wei-ming, T. "The Confucian Perception of Adulthood." In *Adulthood,* edited by E. Erickson, pp. 113–20. New York: Norton, 1978.

White, J. *The Highest State of Consciousness.* New York: Anchor Books, 1972.

Whitehead, A. N. "Autobiographical Notes." In *The Philosophy of Alfred North Whitehead*, edited by P. A. Schilpp, pp. 1 – 14. New York: Tudor, 1941.
—————. *The Concept of Nature*. Cambridge: Cambridge University Press, 1920.
—————. *An Enquiry Concerning the Principles of Natural Knowledge*. Cambridge: Cambridge University Press, 1919.
—————. *Modes of Thought*. New York: Macmillan, 1938.
—————. *Organization of Thought, Educational and Scientific*. London: Williams and Norgate, 1917.
—————. *Religion in the Making*. New York: Macmillan, 1926.
—————. *Science and the Modern World*. New York: Macmillan, 1925.
Whitmont, E. *The Symbolic Quest*. Princeton: Princeton University Press, 1969.
Wilber, K. *The Atman Project: A Transpersonal View of Human Development*. Wheaton, Ill: Quest, 1980.
—————. *No Boundary: Eastern and Western Approaches to Personal Growth*. Boston: Shambhala, 1981.
—————. "The Pre/Trans Fallacy." *ReVision* 5 (1980): 51 – 71.
Woods, N., and Witte, K. "Life Satisfaction, Fear of Death, and Ego Identity in Elderly Adults." *Bulletin of the Psychonomic Society* 18 (1981): 165 – 8.
Yasuda, Y. *Old Tales of Japan*. Tokyo: Tuttle, 1965.
Young, G., and Dowling, W. "Dimensions of Religiosity in Old Age: Accounting for Variation in Type of Participation." *Journal of Gerontology* 42 (1987): 376 – 80.
Zheleznova, I. *Tales of the Amber Sea: Fairy Tales of the Peoples of Estonia, Latvia and Lithuania*. Moscow: Progress Publishers, 1974.
Zinberg, N. E. "The Relationship of Regressive Phenomena to the Aging Process." In *Normal Psychology of the Aging Process*, edited by N. E. Zinberg and I. Kaufman, pp. 143 – 59. New York: International Universities Press, 1961.
—————. "Psychoanalytic Consideration of Aging." *Journal of the American Psychoanalytic Association* 12 (1964): 151 – 9.
Zipes, J. *Breaking the Magic Spell: Radical Theories of Folk and Fairy Tales*. Austin: University of Texas Press, 1979.
—————. *Don't Bet on the Prince: Contemporary Feminist Fairy Tales in North America and England*. New York: Methuen, 1976.
—————. *Fairy Tales and the Art of Subversion: The Classical Genre for Children and the Process of Socialization*. New York: Heinemann, 1983.
Zoja, L. "Working Against Dorian Gray: Analysis and the Old." *Journal of Analytical Psychology* 28 (1983): 51 – 64.

Index